MAGIC AND SUPERSTITION

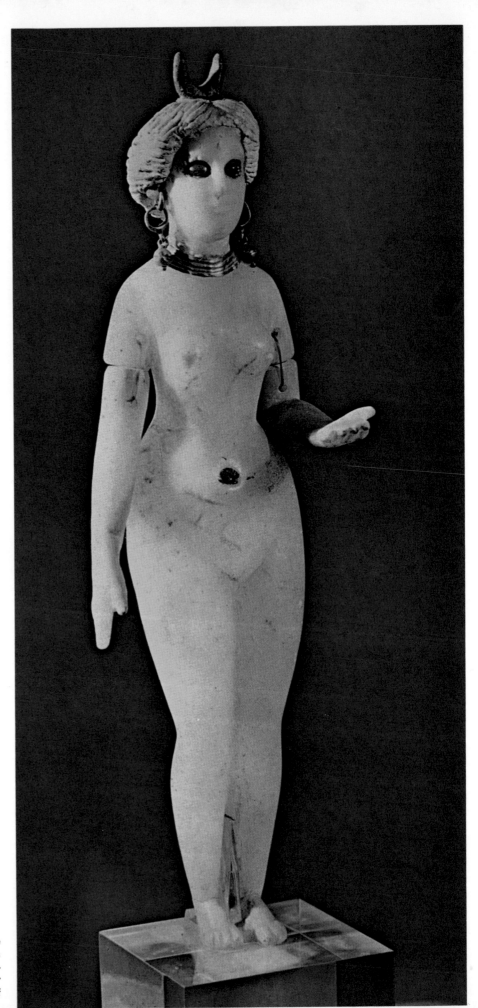

This is an alabaster statue of Astarte, the Mesopotamian goddess of love, and dates from 2000 BC. The crescent-moon head-dress she wears symbolically connects her with supernatural mystery and, because of its resemblance to horns, sexuality.

MAGIC AND SUPERSTITION

DOUGLAS HILL

PAUL HAMLYN

Published 1968 by THE HAMLYN PUBLISHING GROUP LTD
LONDON · NEW YORK · SYDNEY · TORONTO
HAMLYN HOUSE, THE CENTRE, FELTHAM, MIDDLESEX
© Copyright 1968 Douglas Hill
Printed in Italy by Arnoldo Mondadori Editore - Verona

CONTENTS

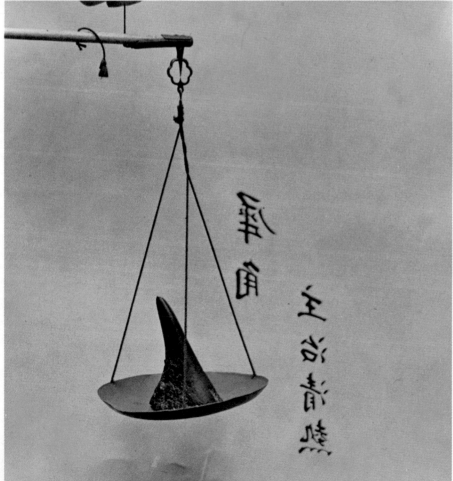

The deer antlers prominent in this Hong Kong shop are eagerly sought by customers wishing to boost their virility.

Like the antlers above, powdered rhino horn is sold by the milligramme, and for the same purpose. Its popularity has led to the near-extinction of the white rhino, which seems to have superseded the unicorn in the popular imagination.

Seven is a number full of magical significance: to find a ladybird with seven spots is a sign of good luck.

THE ORIGINS OF OUR SUPERSTITIONS

Folklore, as one wise folklorist has said, is nothing but history born out of wedlock. So superstition, as a part of folklore, may simply be an equally illegitimate branch of religious history. For the folk beliefs that are to be considered in this book can be gathered together as methods of predicting, avoiding or controlling certain occurrences by *supernatural*, or irrational, means.

This is clearly a definition of magic, as our most primitive ancestors saw it. And it becomes clear that superstition and folk belief are indistinguishable from magic. Many writers cloud the meaning of the word 'superstition' by lumping in with true folk beliefs all the misconceptions and fallacies that spring up around complex, specialized subjects. For instance, it is superstition to believe that rain can be caused by stepping on a spider. It is a fallacy to assume that bad weather is caused by 'all those atom bombs'. The former presupposes an occult, magical connection; the latter presupposes a non-existent *physical* connection between nuclear explosions and the weather of a particular locality. In the same way, one might say, it is superstition to believe that certain numbers (3, 7, 9, etc.) are in themselves lucky; it is fallacious to believe that the figures of statistics ever reveal more than half-truths. It is a superstition to seek to change a politician's ways by muttering incantations over a voodoo doll in his image; it is a misconception to believe he can be swayed by a protest letter to a newspaper.

So in these chapters the subject will be the folk beliefs, the old wives' tales, the childish fears and suppositions based on supernatural lore that have been handed down over generations, or centuries—with apparently little concern for the great many instances that must

have occurred of their failure. Much of the time, of course, the supernatural itself—in its familiar guise of witchcraft, the black arts and so on—may not be overtly apparent. Superstitious folk have often de-supernaturalized (if such a word may be coined) their beliefs— and have replaced the occult with the less compromising euphemism of 'luck'. Luck is a vague, indefinite quality that certain objects possess, and that they can confer on their owners; or luck exists, as it were, in the air around us, sometimes serving us, sometimes avoiding us, sometimes able to be *summoned* to us; and luck is a quality possessed by certain individuals (who are 'born lucky') or races ('the luck of the Irish'— as unfounded a superstition as any, given Ireland's history).

Luck is not the same as chance: it is chance that presents us with alternatives and luck that affects our choice. Luck, which we can sometimes control, or try to, guides us through the chances that present themselves during our lives. The unsuperstitious man tries to arrange his life-pattern so that chance plays as small a part in it as possible; the superstitious 'trust to luck'. Not for nothing has luck been anthropomorphized as a lady: just as we feel that she is with us, that we can understand and dominate her, she proves herself erratic, whimsical, capricious and wholly irrational. She might be there when we need her—if we are lucky.

But the unreliability of luck has never stopped its devotees—who must be not only perennial optimists but also fatalists—from developing more and more magical ways to tie it down. And these techniques of superstition almost invariably take one of three basic forms.

First, the *omens*, the signs and forewarnings by which we claim to

12

Rabbit-foot charms waiting to be despatched from a factory. Ten million of these are sold every year in the United States.

Left: *The Witches*, a woodcut by Hans Baldung, 1510. Here are many motifs common to witchcraft and superstition: cats, magic brews, fire, rams (like the goat, a form often taken by the Devil).

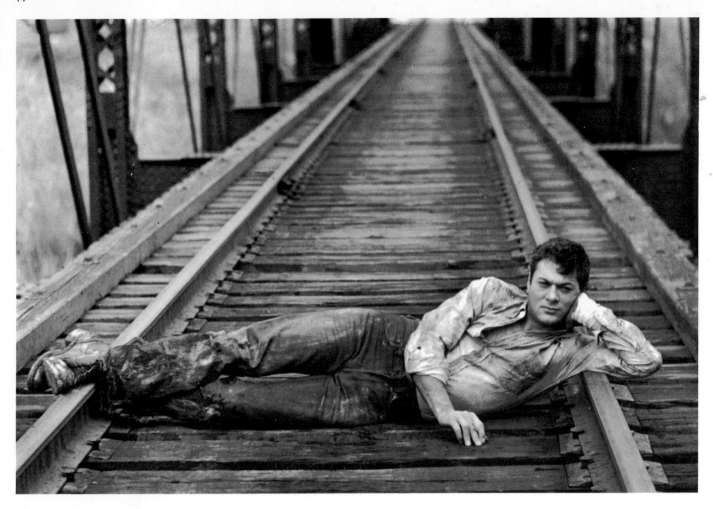

Tony Curtis is said to hold a wide variety of superstitions – including fear of white cats crossing his path, and of the number fourteen.

know that if such-and-such occurs so-and-so will invariably follow. A belief in omens is a belief in a predetermined future, totally fatalistic—that a specific cause will always, automatically, bring about a specific effect. Finding money, or a pin, on the ground is an omen of good luck. An itchy ear is an omen of misfortune, an itchy nose means a visitor coming. A dog following you home is a good omen. A dropped dishcloth presages a pleasant surprise, or a visitor. Stumbling at the beginning of a journey, or a new enterprise, is very ominous. And so on, and so on. At times there are techniques which one can employ to avert the effect, if it is bad luck. But this is fighting magic with magic, and it is unreliable; no one is very surprised when such attempts fail to work.

Secondly, the taboos: *don't* speak certain words, or commit certain actions—otherwise disaster will befall you, in a specific form or in the form of general ill fortune. Taboos, in the primitive supernatural beliefs of which they are an integral part, are forbidden because they will provoke evil spirits, or the inhuman magical 'essence' that pervades every aspect of primitive life,

to assault the infringer. The taboos of more modern superstition make no mention of evil spirits—but they imply that ill fortune is ever-present, just out of sight, waiting to envelop anyone who is unwary enough, say, to walk under a ladder, to open an umbrella indoors, to 'speak of the devil', to step on a crack in the pavement or to shake hands with the left hand. Sometimes taboos, like omens, can be counteracted with swift and positive magical action— but, again, such counteraction is often employed more in hope than in expectation.

Thirdly, the rituals: this is a term that will be applied here to the actions that *should* be performed to bring about specific desirable effects, or to avert bad luck, or to ensure good luck generally. Crossing the fingers is a familiar method of averting evil (forming a cross, of course, drives away devils); children making a wish on birthday-cake candles, or on the first star in the evening, are performing a positive ritual.

The dominating presence of magic in folk belief clearly appears in the latter's use of so many traditionally magical objects and substances. For

William the Conqueror stumbled when he first landed in Britain. To reassure his followers he grasped the earth and claimed that he was taking possession of English soil.

'Bears, bears, look at me treading in all the squares!' Like Christopher Robin, children still avoid cracks in the pavement.

centuries the occult arts, witchcraft, sorcery, divination and so on, have endowed aspects of the natural world with a special power of their own, residing within.

(To the primitive mind, of course, *every* aspect of the environment contains this almost transcendental power, which man can tap or plug into.)

So one can find many uses in superstition for salt, a necessary but sometimes a difficult substance to obtain in ancient times, and thus a constituent of much primitive magic. Cold iron (and in modern times steel) has its magical power, mainly to do good—because witches and demons fear it. Fire, of all the ancient world's four elements of matter, has the strongest supernatural associations, and figures in both good and bad luck beliefs. Numbers are magical in their various ways, as are colours; certain plants and animals are important to witchcraft and also to folk superstition. Stones, various woods, and most metals possess power. The moon, and to a lesser degree the sun and the stars, have their place in superstition over and above their function in astrology.

Parts of the human body—nails, hair, excreta, and especially blood—find their way into the omens and rituals of superstition, because of their intrinsic power and also because of the undying belief in what anthropologists call 'sympathetic' magic. This belief is based on the idea that whatever happens to a part of something, or to an image of it, will be magically caused to happen to the whole, or to the reality. Out of sympathetic magic grow, for example, the unpleasant dolls that witches and black magicians are supposed to make, in order to harm others. If a doll made to represent an individual (preferably containing some of the person's hair or other body dross) is burned, stabbed, or buried, the individual should by rights die the same way—but inexplicably, so far as any onlooker is concerned.

The amulets and talismans carried by primitives to ward off evil have a host of counterparts in folk belief. That old favourite 'lucky piece', the rabbit's foot, is such an amulet, as are the four-leaf clover and the horseshoe. Many people today have chosen, by some irrational procedure, their own private good-luck charms—perhaps a special coin, or decorative charms on bracelets or key-chains.

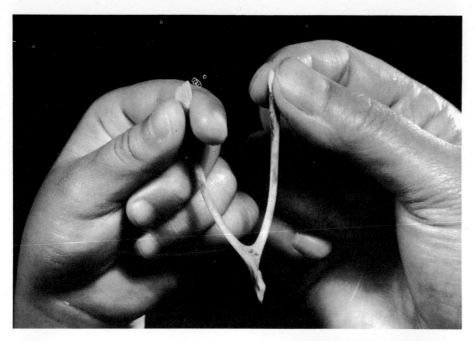

A legend surrounds this 300-year-old trumpet sold in 1967 at Christies for £1,600. It is believed to bring its owner bad luck if it is not blown regularly. Accordingly, a distinguished musicologist was summoned to start the bidding with a fanfare (far left).

To break a wish-bone with someone is an old custom: whoever gets the larger piece gets his wish. Like the horseshoe, the wishbone may once have symbolized the magic powers of the horned moon.

This old woodcut (above) from the year 1525 shows a man extending two fingers, like the horns of Astarte, to ward off the Devil.

Left: 'I'll keep my fingers crossed for you' – once we used to make the form of a cross to keep the Devil at bay.

If one blows out the candles in one puff, one's wish is granted. Note the candles, horseshoe and cross-shaped cake: they are all lucky symbols.

Even in a busy street, people will avoid ladders: many people who claim *not* to be superstitious still won't walk under them (far left).

18

All these hoary old elements of magic will appear from time to time in the chapters that follow, in terms of particular aspects of superstition. So, in many cases, the *origin* of folk beliefs can be traced back to the lore of sorcery and magic that inhabited men's minds from the Stone Age onwards. And, in fact, the true beginnings of much present-day superstition lie buried among the primeval foliage. Other superstitions, which may seem to have been born in modern times, appear on closer examination to be merely ancient beliefs rigged out in modern dress. Still others, more localized perhaps, may have grown out of local misobservation and may thus have become hallowed by legend and tradition within an isolated community. For instance, if in some backwoods district John Brown had a hawk's nest on his barn and the barn burned down, hawks nesting on buildings might be an omen of bad luck in that district. Even so, the belief will usually have clear parallels and analogues within the mainstream of magic and witchcraft in the way that has been discussed.

Because so much of superstition has existed for centuries as an oral tradition, passed along by osmosis from father to son (or, more accurately perhaps, from granny to nervous children), origin-tracing generally seems impossible. Nevertheless, some expert folklorists from time to time can determine if not the origin at least the *background*, the family tree as it were, of certain beliefs. Some of these suggestions seem more to be inspired guesses than hard fact, but make rich food for thought. In succeeding chapters, whenever possible, the ground that nurtured specific beliefs will be indicated. Here, it may

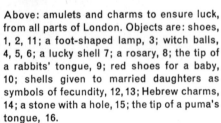

Above: amulets and charms to ensure luck, from all parts of London. Objects are: shoes, 1, 2, 11; a foot-shaped lamp, 3; witch balls, 4, 5, 6; a lucky shell 7; a rosary, 8; the tip of a rabbits' tongue, 9; red shoes for a baby, 10; shells given to married daughters as symbols of fecundity, 12, 13; Hebrew charms, 14; a stone with a hole, 15; the tip of a puma's tongue, 16.

Performers in a Benin rite, dancing on ropes hanging from a sacred tree. Here again we find wood, or the spirit of the tree, being revered and used in rituals.

be worthwhile taking some of the most familiar superstitions in the modern world and looking at their ancestry in this way.

The foot of the lowly rabbit brings comfort and reassurance to millions throughout the world, in the form of handy charms for pocket, jewellery, key chain or car keys. Logically, the rabbit's foot should be associated with the idea of speed and flight; the rabbit itself seems to be used in colloquial metaphor as an image of cowardice, mildness, and a form of uninhibited but rather immature sexuality.

Yet in magical belief there is a direct connection between the rabbit (and its cousin the hare) and witchcraft. Witches, numbering among their powers the ability to change shape, were believed often to take the form of rabbits. Thus for some groups of people —fishermen and sailors especially, as Chapter 4 will show—rabbits were creatures of ill omen. But at the same time in northern Europe the rabbit has come to be associated with spring, and the theme of renewal—hence its presence in our secular Easter celebrations. Linked with this idea, again, is the

Dr John Dee and Edward Kelly conjuring a ghost. This is the frontispiece for *Histoire Curieuse et Pittoresque des Sorciers*, by Mathias de Giraldo, Paris 1840. Like many superstitious rites this occurs at midnight in a graveyard, with appropriate symbols.

Here are rabbits' feet being cut to size before being dried and dyed for use as good-luck charms (far left).

Ancient Britons near a sacred wood (from an eighteenth-century print, left). The oak tree, iron sickle, mistletoe and grave-stones all had ritual significance, and many of these motifs still survive in European folk belief – for instance, we still say 'touch wood'.

The bunny-girl has a long history: rabbits and eggs have always been linked with fertility, so why not get one to deliver the other at Easter? When children hunt for them, they continue an old adult rite.

A Zulu medicine man: he wears horn amulets for protection and power.

Horseshoes are traditionally lucky, especially if they have seven nails. Usually they are hung with the ends pointing upwards, to stop the luck running out.

Smiths were thought to possess special powers because of their association with fire and iron: hence, perhaps, one reason for the popularity of weddings at Gretna Green, conducted on a smith's anvil.

Bette Davis seldom goes anywhere without her lucky charm bracelet. Once it fell overboard at the start of a European tour, and she refused to leave until a longshoreman had recovered it.

The luck of the Irish is perpetuated every St Patrick's Day by the distribution of shamrocks: this three-leaved plant is associated with the Holy Trinity, and thus is very lucky.

rabbit's undeniable fecundity, which made it an obvious fertility symbol. It is not much of a step from that to the belief that a rabbit, or parts of one, could confer fertility—in which one can include everything from sexual potency to financial prosperity to general good luck. Feet have a certain symbolic association with sex—as any good Freudian knows—and so eventually this part of the rabbit came to be popularized in folk belief as the repository of good fortune. Of course, many folk beliefs concerning the whole rabbit remain extant: for instance, in parts of Britain, a rabbit confers good luck by crossing your path in front of you, bad luck by crossing behind. And a rabbit running past a house foretells a fire. In terms of the foot again,

its luck-bringing potential is increased if it is the left hind foot (the left side being the 'sinister', irrational side); some people, with varying degrees of mockery, have added that the rabbit should be killed at the full of the moon, or in the dark of the moon, in a cemetery by a red-haired, cross-eyed man or woman.

Another old favourite, the horseshoe, is made of iron, which is regarded as an infallible witch repellent. It is vaguely in the shape of the new moon—the horned crescent—which is highly powerful; it has also been seen as a female sexual symbol. The best horseshoes have four nails on one side and three on the other, and the number seven is almost universally lucky. And horseshoes are (or were) made by black-

smiths, who were for centuries believed to have special powers due to their work with fire and iron. Horses themselves have a place in magic—having been sacred beasts in many cultures, ridden by gods and heroes, and symbolic of fertility and virility. Thus they confer extra power on the shoes (as well as on blacksmiths).

A horseshoe is especially lucky if it has been found on the road, and, in Britain, if it has been cast from the near hind-leg of a grey mare. Despite the fact that many modern people prefer imitation shoes in this horseless age, often small plastic shoes on a charm bracelet, purists will insist that only the real thing has power. Usually horseshoes are nailed up over doorways, to keep off evil; and the majority

22

The Balder myth (right) is one source of the unpopularity of the number 13. Thirteen people were present when Loki killed the handsome Balder, who was protected from every wood except mistletoe. Loki knew this and during a game handed a piece to Hod (who was blind), who threw it in fun at Balder; he died instantly.

The United States Seal, ignoring the omen, contains no fewer than 8 groups of 13, representing the original 13 States.

Consternation in the household: 13 at table! Even the maid looks aghast!

of people insist that the points must be upwards, so that the shoe forms a U, and does not 'spill the luck' or let it 'run out'.

Four-leafed clovers draw most of their power from the mystical connotations of the number four, which, in numerology and mythology, appears constantly as a symbol of balance, unity and completeness. The number three has also had lucky connotations—especially in the Christian era, due to association with the Trinity. Thus a normally three-leafed plant, lucky in itself and so useful in keeping off supernatural evil (hence the emblem of the Irish shamrock), would have its power immensely increased with the addition

of another leaf. The four-leaf clover's comparative rarity assists its aura of luckiness: although horticulturalists can now breed them at will, to satisfy demand. And in parts of Britain a five-leaf clover brings financial luck, a six-leaf clover confers fame (sometimes the gift of prophecy), and one with seven leaves brings immeasurable good luck and protection from all mishaps and evil—even from violent death.

From some well-known amulets and talismans, we pass to some well-known omens and taboos. Pride of place can be given to the number thirteen, around which a crushing load of superstitious fear has gathered. Today most people think that 'triskaideka-

Far left: it is unlucky to spill salt; but one can guard against bad luck by throwing a pinch over one's left shoulder with the right hand – presumably to frighten the Devil, who is traditionally associated with the left, or sinister, side.

London's Savoy Hotel keeps a lucky black cat to occupy an extra seat if 13 people arrive for any function. This was designed in 1926 by Basil Ionides, and adorns Churchill's favourite Pinafore Room.

This woodcut from the Lübeck Bible (1494) shows Jacob's Ladder, which is one of the ladder's main mystical associations. By passing under one, it is thought that a triangle (an ancient symbol of life), or trinity, will be broken, bringing bad luck.

phobia', the fear of thirteen, grew out of the fact that thirteen sat down at the Last Supper. But in fact the superstition is far older. In Norse mythology, twelve gods were gathered at a feast when Loki, the red-haired evil-doer and spirit of strife, entered—and there developed a dispute that ended with the death of Balder, the favourite of the gods. The Romans disliked thirteen, in their numerological fortune-telling, regarding it as a sign of destruction. In slightly more recent times, the number has always had unpleasant associations: in the days of witch hunts, the witches' covens were supposedly composed of thirteen members.

"E's awful superstitious, wouldn't dream of workin' any week wi' a Friday in it either."

At the beginning of the 1952 Olympic Games, in Helsinki, white doves were released. A dove brought Noah the first news of dry land, and it is a form often taken by the Holy Spirit. Moreover, doves were used as birds of sacrifice in many ancient religions. Thus these birds, especially white ones, have come to symbolize peace and friendship.

Maxine Morris, self-styled 'Queen of England's 30,000 witches' and technical adviser for the film 'The Eye of the Devil', performs the ritual of 'calling down the moon'. Note the prominence of Hebrew magical emblems as well as pagan elements like the knife and circle.

Thirteen is especially unlucky in terms of dinner parties, referring back to the Last Supper or the Norse feast: it is believed that one of the thirteen diners will die within a year. But the fear exists in every occurrence of the number. Throughout the western world people can still be found numbering their houses '12½', to avoid living in number 13. The state lotteries of France, Italy, and elsewhere never sell tickets with that number. Hotels and hospitals, and similar institutions, often have no room numbered thirteen; and many big hotels, like the new Cavendish Hotel completed in London in 1966, also have no thirteenth floor. Fear is also aroused if the thirteenth of the month falls on a Friday—

itself a notoriously unlucky day, largely by association with Good Friday.

Salt is a powerful magical substance, as has been indicated; thus the spilling of salt is a dangerous omen. The substance itself is venerated because it is unchanging, and because it preserves other things, such as meat, from decay; hence it became a symbol of eternity and immutability. From primeval times it has played a part in ceremonies and rituals—especially those marking some form of pledge. 'Taking salt together' binds two men in eternal friendship. It was often included in sacrifices designed to propitiate gods or spirits. And it has been used as a means of keeping devils and witches away. Many people today still carry a pinch of salt

as a talisman bringing good fortune. An old British tradition states that salt should be among the gifts brought to a new baby; and that salt should be left behind when one moves house. Above all, it is a bad omen to spill salt: it must not be scraped up, but a pinch should be thrown over the left shoulder as a ritual means of counteracting evil. But salt itself is not entirely a beneficial magic: tears are saline, and the superstitious tendency to associative magic has produced the old wives' saying, 'Help me to salt, help me to sorrow'.

Primitive man, believing in the abiding presence of sympathetic magic, drew no clear dividing line between the image of something and the reality. So the image of a man contained a portion of his life-essence—even the mirror image. Mirrors gained in this way some sanctity, and breaking a mirror could injure or destroy the man who at the time was looking into it. Eventually the fear of broken mirrors was extended: today it is widely believed that breaking a mirror, whether or not one is looking into it, presages bad luck. Some say seven years' bad luck, which limitation dates from Roman numerological belief. A related but today less prevalent superstition exists— that it is harmful to a man to step on or otherwise interfere with his shadow, which is also an image that contains something of his soul.

Superstitious folk fear walking under ladders, not because they are worried that something might be dropped on them, but because ladders have long been symbols of a spiritual ascent to heaven. One must detour around them

This Kano witch-doctor sells specially prepared bones, skins, shells, dead birds and
snakes for implementing spells.

Seen here (right) with President Johnson at his inauguration of the baseball season is Senator Margaret Chase Smith. She is never seen without a rose, which appears to be a personal superstition.

Witches were thought to offer their children to the Devil. This woodcut, produced during the trial of Agnes Sampson, 1591, perpetuated the myth.

Dora Bryan and other members of the cast of 'Hello Dolly' celebrate the show's first anniversary with a cake, for good luck. Anniversary and birthday cakes probably originate from the customary sacrifices to the gods at important stages of one's life (right).

to avoid disturbing—and drawing the wrath of—any spirits that might be using them. Also, a ladder leaning against a wall forms a triangle, a symbol of life in ancient times. It is dangerous to walk through, and therefore break, the symbol. (If one *must* walk under a ladder, the evil can be offset by crossing the fingers, or spitting over the left shoulder, or remaining silent until some four-legged animal is seen.)

In America, Canada and many European countries including Belgium and Spain, black cats are considered especially ill-omened. In Britain, however, black cats are omens of good luck. This opposition is the most striking inconsistency in all international superstition, probably because the black-cat

fear still thrives while some other inconsistencies have faded. Of course the supernatural association of the cat itself hardly needs elaboration: cats were worshipped in magic-riddled Egypt, were sacred to the Roman goddess Diana, were the favourite forms of witches' familiars, or shape-changing witches themselves, in the Middle Ages. A black cat, a doubly mysterious, eerie, nocturnal creature, would naturally be associated with the dark forces of evil. But the individualistic British, for whom *white* cats are unlucky, seem to view black ones exactly as the ancient Egyptians did—with reverence—as if the witchcraft associations had had no effect on the belief.

A common evil-averting ritual, used mainly when someone has been speak-

27

Anthony Perkins is said to believe, like many of us, that is is unlucky if one's shoe-laces become undone – so he never wears shoes with laces.

These members of the 13 Club couldn't care less about ladders – or broken mirrors! They meet regularly on Fridays, and dine with 13 at table, for the express purpose of breaking as many taboos as possible.

ing highly of himself or expressing hopes for the future, requires him to touch wood—or knock on it. Thus he avoids tempting fate—or rather tempting evil spirits to puncture his pride or hopes by depriving him of his good fortune. The ritual probably has its roots in ancient primitive times, when many trees and their wood were sacred, holy and very powerful. Such wood could be brandished, or merely touched, to hold off evil. (Touching iron has the same effect, but has been less long-lived—because the wood-touching ritual gained extra strength through association with the holy wood of the cross.)

The taboo against opening an umbrella indoors is thought, by 'sensible' people, to be simply a way of avoiding

breakages among the bric-à-brac of interior decoration. But there is also a clear connection with an ancient belief in the mystical power of the sun: umbrellas, in their original form of parasols or sun-shades, held a special magical relationship with the sun, being in effect the sun's 'property'. Hence, opening a parasol indoors, or anywhere out of the sun's rays, was dangerously offensive to the sun-spirit.

Another taboo, against lighting three cigarettes on one match, is often thought to have a modern practical basis. It is said that in wartime, especially in the trench warfare of World War I, a sniper spotting a match flame would have time to take aim and kill the owner of the third cigarette. But in fact this belief considerably antedates

the twentieth century: it is related to the old Christian fear of offending against the Trinity. Also, in the Russian Orthodox church, three candles were traditionally lit by the priest, from one taper, at funerals—and the sombre association was transferred into folk belief. Some authorities suggest that the practice of lighting three flames at funeral rites goes back to pagan times, which would give this superstition a considerable pedigree.

Knives have gathered much lore around them, largely because in the primitive past they were as basic a part of a man's everyday equipment as, say, shoes are today. Knives made of iron or steel naturally take on the magical value of that metal in repelling evil. But today the most common

Girl's death in legend of curse

FROM OUR CORRESPONDENT—New York, Dec. 14

Miss Evalyn McLean, former joint heiress to the Hope diamond and its reputed curse, was found dead last night at her home in a suburb of Dallas, Texas, where she lived alone. A post mortem examination showed no indication of violence; an analysis of stomach contents is to be made.

Neighbours broke into the house after seeing no activity for several days, and found the body, dressed in blue jeans and sweater, on a bed.

Miss McLean, 25, a former Dallas debutante, quiet-living, was the granddaughter of the late Evalyn Walsh McLean, who said that she paid $40,000 (then £8,000) for the Hope diamond about 60 years ago.

She left it jointly to her six grandchildren when she died in 1947. A dealer bought it from the estate in 1949 and gave it to the Smithsonian Institution in Washington. The grandchildren were never allowed to touch it.

The Hope diamond turned up in London in 1812 and got its name from Henry Thomas Hope, an English banker who bought it in 1830. The story is that the 44½-carat stone was ripped from the forehead

Evalyn McLean : Dead in house.

of an Indian idol, and came into the hands of a French traveller who was later torn to death by a pack of rabid dogs.

Louis XIV of France is said to have given it to Mme. de Montespan as a mark of royal favour, which she lost soon after.

Louis XVI, the legend says, gave it to Marie Antoinette and it disappeared when they were executed in 1793.

As far as Mrs. Evalyn Walsh McLean was concerned, her first son was killed in a car accident, her husband died in a mental home, and a daughter died of an overdose of sleeping pills in 1946.

The Hope family is said to have fallen on evil days after buying the diamond, and the catalogue of owners in the 16 years before Mrs. McLean includes Jacques Colet, who killed himself, Prince Ivan Kanitovitsky, who was murdered, Sultan Abdul Hamid of Turkey, who was dethroned, and a mistress who was murdered; and Simon Montharides, whose carriage was dragged over a cliff by a shying horse killing himself, his wife and their child.

This account of the Hope Diamond curse appeared in *The Times*, 15 December 1967.

In the picture opposite Goya shows witches offering babies to the Devil. The crescent moon, bats, oak-wreath and goat-like form are traditional black-magic associations.

---

superstition concerns the gift of a knife from one friend to another: some fear that the cutting edge will symbolically sever the friendship. As a counter-ritual the recipient must give something in return—usually a small coin—so that he will seem to be buying the knife, which is not taboo.

Not many people realize that the tendency to comment on someone's sneeze—usually with a variant on 'Bless you!'—is in fact a magical act. The blessing has little to do with a friendly hope that the sneezer is not catching cold. It actually stems from the primitive belief that a man's soul can leave his body through the mouth, and that a sneeze may thus expel it, leaving it vulnerable to evil influences. The blessing is a counteracting ritual. (The soul was often thought to slip out during sleep as well, for which reason primitives dislike awakening a sleeper suddenly—in case his soul cannot get back in time. From this idea descends the common notion, still current but quite baseless, that it is unwise suddenly to awaken a sleepwalker.)

A parallel to the belief that the soul is contained in a sneeze is the idea that one's breath has some magical virtue, drawn from one's life-essence. Hence gamblers, for instance, blow on their cards or dice to improve their luck. Saliva also has its share of the same power: simple spitting is a common ritual to bring good luck. Lucky charms are spat upon to increase their potency. And men will sometimes spit on their hands before beginning manual work (with a spade, axe, etc.), perhaps thinking they do so to improve their grip, but in fact following an age-old ritual to make their work easier.

The chapters that follow will present many more superstitions and folk beliefs (along with their magical relationships and, where possible, hints as to their origins) that are found in the most important aspects of human life. Some of them will be old beliefs that have now pretty well died out. But a great many can be found flourishing in the modern world—in spite of our often self-satisfied claim to be more rational, sceptical, science-oriented, than ever.

To indicate just how endemic—or pandemic—superstition remains, and to conclude this introductory chapter, here are a few facts and instances.

In ultra-modern New York, shops that cater to magic and superstition seem to grow increasingly numerous. They sell the usual lucky charms and amulets, and also materials for charms and spells that smack of the witches' chant in *Macbeth*. The cost of a newt's eye is not known to us, but a few years ago you could buy a vial of graveyard dust for fifty cents, a 'hexing' candle for a dollar, and a 'coin from a corpse's eye' for ten dollars.

In 1965, also in New York, the peacocks that decorated the lawns of the United Nations building were removed. They were reported to have made some delegates (unidentified) ill-at-ease. Peacock feathers, with their eye-like design, have long been associated with the legend of the 'evil eye'.

In 1962, in Britain, a manufacturer suffered a loss when he made the error of sending out *green* hot-water bottles to the shops. People would not buy

Mirrors have always played a role in magical lore. At first it was believed that one could make magic with a man's shadow in order to harm him. Then they became associated with vanity and the Devil himself. 'Frailty thy name is woman', preaches this mediaeval woodcut: the Devil seems to agree.

them. Green is traditionally an unlucky colour, especially in Celtic tradition where it is associated with the 'Little People'.

In 1963, the newly formed Federation of Malaysia celebrated its birth by ceremonies that included the release of 101 white pigeons. The birds are traditionally omens of peace and good luck; the number in numerology is also lucky.

In 1960 a British educationist conducted a small experiment—setting up a ladder against a wall, over a narrow sidewalk that ran along an extremely busy street. Over 70 per cent of the people who passed that way—including clergymen and policemen—stepped off the sidewalk, risking the traffic rather than walk under the ladder.

In 1965 British Gas Board officials revealed that mothers were walking their children around the gasworks in one area, making the circuit three times at night—in a folk-medicine cure for whooping cough.

In 1960 in New Jersey, USA, ground-breaking ceremonies were planned to begin the work on a new bridge costing $1,250,000. But the ceremonies had to be cancelled: someone had arranged them for a Friday, and too many people were upset at the likelihood of bad luck.

In 1966, an American businessman visiting an industrial plant in Japan found to his horror that the plant was still producing parts—some $30,000 worth—for a contract that the American's firm had cancelled at the beginning of that year. The Japanese explained that there was no mistake, but that it was very unlucky for business to have a contract cancelled on the first day of the year—so they had ritually pretended to continue it.

It was estimated, some years ago, that superstitious America spends about $125,000,000 yearly on forms of fortune telling and divination. About 10,000,000 rabbits' feet are sold in the USA annually, and about four million four-leafed clovers. Nor is there any reason to suppose that these figures have diminished today. Another estimate states that every Friday 13th costs America about $250,000,000 in lost business—because where possible people will stay at home, not shopping or travelling or taking risks at all.

Unquestionably, a great many modern people include various forms of

The snake has always been an equivocal symbol. Although, since Genesis, the Christian symbol of evil, it has also been a classical symbol of healing.

Below, right: the famous magician Nostradamus shows Catherine of France the succession of monarchs in his magic mirror. After Louis XIV, Jesuits were going to abolish the monarchy, he said.

Overleaf: these Hallowe'en masks are reminders that the spirits of the dead rise on All Hallows Eve: magicians casting spells on this night of witchery must wear masks to avoid being recognized by evil spirits.

superstition in their normal patterns of everyday life, but at the same time they would never consciously or publicly admit to being superstitious. A British psychologist, Peter McKellar, has used the term 'half belief' for this widespread attitude: the half-believers, seeing themselves as rational beings, will intellectually reject superstition, and thus will claim that they carry a rabbits' foot just for the fun of it, or that they touch wood as a joke. But that they perform these actions at all is revealing. Somehow they are playing safe, hedging their bets, refusing entirely to reject the possibility that there might be 'something in it' after all, that luck may be in some way controllable. We may not be as superstition-dominated as our ancestors; but as long as this propensity to an irrational half-belief exists, the old wives' tales, the omens and taboos and rituals will continue to find fertile growing ground. Man is in part an irrational creature, and from his irrationality spring many magnificent things—most of his art, much of his science and philosophy, all of his religion. Perhaps the fact that superstitions thrive in the same soil is, after all, a fairly small price to pay.

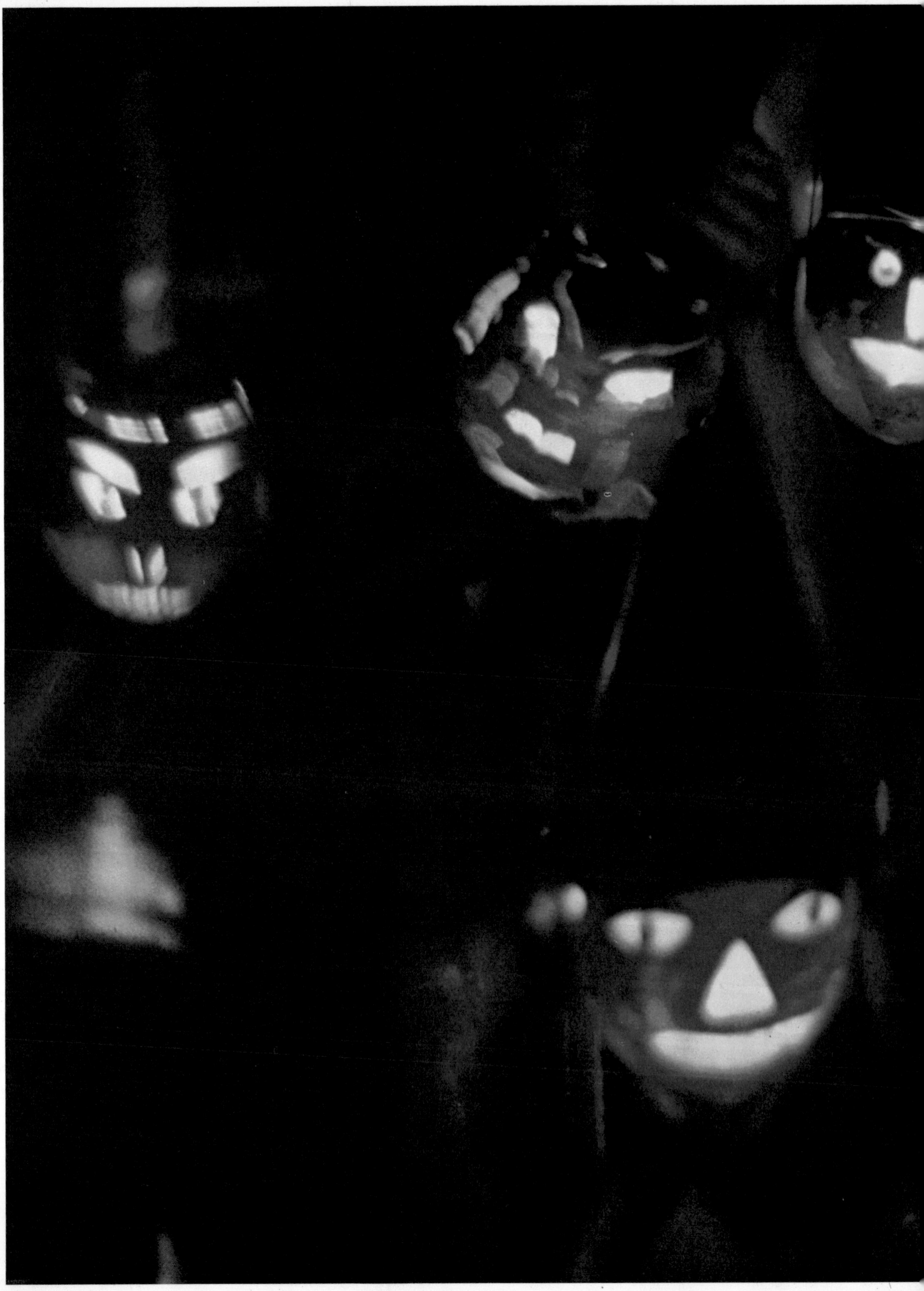

THE CUSTOMS AND MAGIC OF LOVE

Superstitious beliefs gather abundantly along every step of a young person's way through the stages of love, courtship, marriage, and child-bearing. And no other area of life (except perhaps illness) seems to have collected so many overtly magical *rituals*—practices designed expressly to provoke certain desired ends. In the realm of courtship especially, good fortune seems to be not so much automatic and predestined as controllable and changeable, by means of pure sorcery.

But then nobody (at least, no man) would deny that a young woman, wholeheartedly determined not to be left on the shelf, applying all the available wiles and techniques of her sex to promote, subtly, her marriage chances, always has something of the sorceress about her. And, if the *salons* of hairdressers and couturiers prove insufficiently magical, folklore provides its own beauty hints. For instance, girls should cut their hair at the time of the new moon, according to a widespread belief, to make it grow luxuriantly; and they should never cut it at the dark of the moon, or it will grow dull and become prematurely grey. Similarly, girls must never cut their hair in March: not only will it become lifeless, but they will also suffer from headaches. And cutting hair at night is said to reduce a girl's sexuality.

Many similar practices exist to better the marital chances of less attractive girls, some requiring a definite hardihood: for instance, the touch of a dead man's hand is widely thought to cure skin blemishes. But often mere beautification will seem too indirect a route to the altar. More valuable, then, are those magical means of causing someone to love you—which work, presumably, whatever you look like. Boys and girls together can choose from a variety of charms, spells and potions.

A charm once current in the Balkans directed a girl to take earth on which the young man of her choice has stepped, put it in a pot, and plant a marigold in it. As the flower bloomed, the young man would love her. (The magical properties of the marigold, a flower that follows the sun and therefore partakes of its power, are well known throughout Europe; its blossoms are often used in wedding bouquets and, distilled, in folk medicines.) It is said in many places that a girl can capture a man's love by stealing his hatband and wearing it as a garter.

Amulet-like objects, containing magic within them, can also be brought to bear: girls from the Ozark hills in the USA carry the beard of a wild turkey to attract love; Texas girls have been said to secrete horned toads about their persons; elsewhere, a girl might hide a rooster's tail-feather in her glove, then shake hands with the man she wants. In each case there is a clear male symbolism or association.

Desperate would-be lovers can resort to more gruesome sorcery, and tap the power that is supposed to rest in the dead. In Ireland, at one time, a boy could steal a hair from a girl's head, thread it on a needle, and pass the needle through a corpse's arm or leg—and the girl would find him irre-

'He loves me... he loves me not...
he loves me...'

Many of the evil associations clustering around the number thirteen stem from the fact that there were thirteen present at the Last Supper (seen above in Leonardo da Vinci's fresco in Milan).

The Devil and his agents can be summoned by name in some rites: ever since the days of ancient Egypt it has been believed that to utter a person's name gave you power to summon them ('Speak of the Devil'). Thus lovers too can be influenced by incantations. Some of the names for the Devil and his henchmen appear on the right.

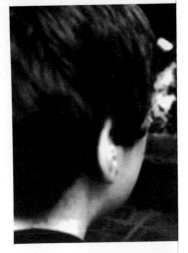

are those potions containin[...]
principle of sympathetic ma[...]
portion of the giver's body[...]
parts of the world it is said[...]
need simply give the man of[...]
a drink in which, earlier[...]
soaked her finger-nail clippi[...]
recipes recommend, instead,[...]
menstrual blood. And an ol[...]
belief directs a man to cu[...]
finger and put a drop of[...]
into the girl's drink.

But perhaps these tech[...]
forcing love may have s[...]
too bold for the shy maid[...]

This Swedish rock painting dates from the Bronze Age, perhaps 3,000 years ago. Much like present-day aborigines, these men seem to be stabbing the ground to increase its fertility. The holes are thought to be either sun-sacrifices, or symbols of women.

We throw rice or confetti over a bride, hoping this will transfer the earth's fertility to her. Conversely, these aborigines at Milingimbi, Northern Australia, are treating the earth like a bride as they stab it with their spears in this fertility ritual.

LUCIFUGÉ , prem. Ministr.

LUCIFER, Empereur.

FLEURETY , lieutenantgén.

SATANACHIA , grand général.

BELZÉBUT, Prince.

SARGATANAS , brigadier.

AGALIAREPT. , aussi général.

ASTAROT , Grand-duc.

NEBIROS , mar. de camp.

This Swedish Midsummer Festival [...]
vival of much older fertility rites: t[...]
maypole and green garlands remain[...]
the purpose has now changed.

sistible. For the girl, a v[...]
practice in Europe and A[...]
quires her to take a needl[...]
been stabbed into a corps[...]
with dirt from an occupied [...]
wrap the whole in cloth fro[...]
ing sheet to make a very [...]
love charm.

Love spells, of course, a[...]
involving verbal incantat[...]
many of them include the [...]
loved one's name—reflectin[...]
old belief (found in most relig[...]
itive and modern) in the [...]
ural power that resides in [...]

gentleman; of white linen, a clergy-man; of darkness, a lawyer; of noises, a tradesman or labourer; of thunder, a soldier or sailor; of rain, a servant. This use of nuts harks back to their ancient role as fertility symbols: they were given to newlyweds in ancient Rome, and are still so given in parts of Europe today. Other love divina-tions employ nuts: for instance, a girl may place chestnuts on the fire, name them for the boys she knows, and the first to pop will indicate the boy she will marry.

'Naming' rituals are widely favoured as divinatory methods. A girl may write the names of three boy-friends on slips of paper, and place them be-neath her pillow. Before going to sleep she removes and discards one slip; immediately upon awakening she re-moves another; the name remaining is that of her husband-to-be. Or she might name the corners of the bedroom (some rituals specify a strange bed-room, when she is away from home): and the corner she is looking at upon awakening represents the boy she will marry.

The initials of a young person's true love can be discovered by catching a snail on Hallowe'en and shutting it up in a flat dish overnight. Next morn-ing, its slime trail is supposed to have traced out the lover's initial. Or a girl can peel an apple without breaking the peel, and throw the peel backwards over her left shoulder. (The left, in folklore, is always the side of magical conjuring.) The peel should then form the initial.

Some of this marriage magic is ac-tually supposed to call up an *appari-tion* of the future spouse. In one exam-ple, found in many countries, a girl stands before a mirror on Hallowe'en, combing her hair with one hand and eating an apple with the other—and her future husband's face will appear in the mirror over her left shoulder. Again, on another magical day—1 May —a girl must go to a well at noon and with a mirror reflect light into the water. In the reflection she may see her husband's face, or she may see nothing at all, a prediction of spin-sterhood. If she sees an image of her-self in a coffin, she will die within the year.

By far the most complex piece of divination involving apparitions goes under the name of the 'dumb (or si-lent) supper', in which a group of girls together conjure up images of their husbands-to-be. The ritual admits of many variations, but in all of them the girls must maintain total silence. Usually the girls bake bread or cake, divide it equally, and sit down to ta-ble to eat it—preferably at midnight. In one version, they then take them-selves to bed, often walking backwards, to dream of their husbands. In another, they set an extra place beside each girl, and put a portion of the cake on each of these plates. Then a cold wind will rise, and the apparitions of the hus-bands will enter to eat their share. Again, a girl may see something she did not bargain for: a black, faceless figure, signifying her imminent death, or simply no one, indicating that she

will not marry. In an old British ver-sion of this rite, the girls set no extra plates, but eat alone; then they loosen all fastenings in their clothes, remove all pins, and go up to bed. Whereupon the apparitions enter and pursue them upstairs, grasping at them. But, because the girls can slip out of their clothing when it is clutched, they can escape.

Many rituals are designed for creat-ing a situation in which the girl meets her future husband in the flesh. If a girl finds a pod holding nine peas, she hangs it over the door, and the first eligible man to enter will marry her. If she finds a four-leaf clover, she can also hang it over her door for the same result, or she can place it in her shoe, in which case the first man she meets while wearing the shoe will be her husband. A girl can pluck twelve leaves of sage at noon on St Mark's Day (25 April), taking one at each stroke of the clock, and the first bachelor she sees she will marry. Or she might pick a rosebud on Midsummer Day, wrap it in white paper and keep it till Christmas Day. At that time it should still be fresh (if not, the portents are ominous); she should wear it to church, where her husband-to-be will come and take it from her. Again, a girl can count seven stars on seven successive nights: the first eligible man she meets (or shakes hands with) on the eighth day will marry her.

This last ritual leaves room for a certain amount of cheating, through conscious control. A girl can simply stay indoors, avoiding everyone except her immediate family, until the boy-

In Keats' poem, the hero takes advantage of the legend surrounding St Agnes' Eve, which says that a woman will dream of her future husband on that night. Porphyro manages to get into his lady's chamber and 'appears' at midnight, as she wakes (far left). They elope.

These Irishwomen are throwing apple-peel into water on Hallowe'en, in the hope that it will form the initials of their future husband. Hallowe'en is named after All Hallows, or All Souls' Day, when the souls of the dead were supposed to stir abroad.

These children are ducking for apples at a Hallowe'en party. Originally, each person placed an apple in the bowl, and you were thought to marry the person whose apple you 'ducked', or managed to bite.

Here an aborigine from Milingimbi, Northern Australia, is collecting his own blood to make magic with, in order to ensure his own fertility.

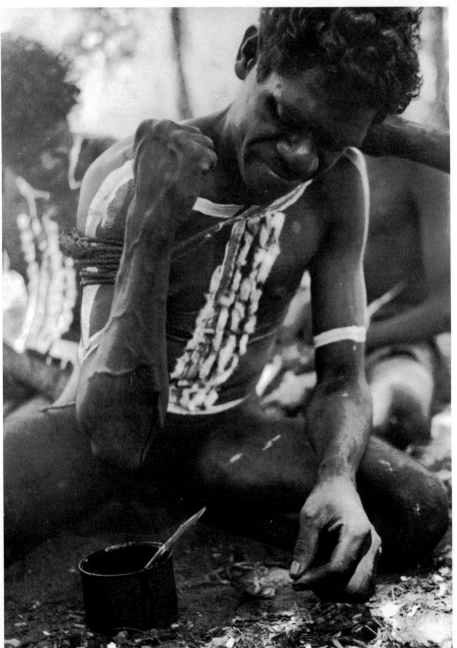

With horseshoes, horse-brasses and a lucky
sweep, this couple on the right should have
all the luck in the world!

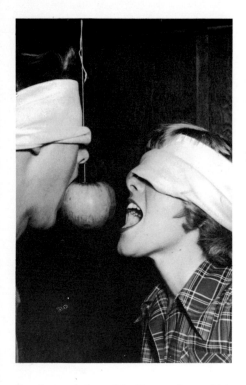

Another variation of ducking apples – which
seem to have been connected with love ever
since Adam and Eve.

friend of her preference comes within
range.

These practices have undoubtedly
worked, by arrangement, on numerous
occasions. And this may explain their
vast popularity—this and the fact that
many of them seem to be little more
than children's time-passing counting
games. There are innumerable variations on the theme of 'count one hundred white horses, and the next man
you meet will become your husband'.
Sometimes the counting task became
even more Herculean—and remains so
in these days when cars have replaced
horses in superstition as elsewhere.
American high school students say
that a girl must count one hundred red
convertibles, then look for a red-headed
woman in a purple dress, then for a
man with a green tie. The first boy to
speak to her after all that will marry
her. But could any girl wait that long?

In France today, a girl must look
for one hundred cars with the number
'21' in their licence plates. Similarly
the girls in Illinois are said to watch
for car licences containing numbers in
groups of three, that is, 000, 111, 222,
up to 999. And the triads must be
found consecutively: an 888 spotted

before a 777 does not count. Once that
hurdle is crossed, the girl then looks
for three white horses and then for a
bald-headed man. The first eligible
man she meets thereafter will become
her husband—if she has not already
passed a marriageable age.

Popular superstitions indicate that
many girls, getting their priorities
straight, seem less interested in learning
whom they will marry, and more in
merely *whether* they will marry, and
how soon. Rituals exist for these ques-
tions too: for instance, a poignant
rhyme (from the American South)
can be spoken by the country girl
who has gone to the woods after
dark:

> If I am to marry near
> Let me hear a bird cry.
> If I am to marry far
> Let me hear a cow low.
> If I am to single die
> Let me hear a knocking by.

But an abundance of simple omens
also exist to reveal whether or not
marriage will take place. Two forks
laid inadvertently beside a plate, or
two teaspoons in a saucer, indicate a

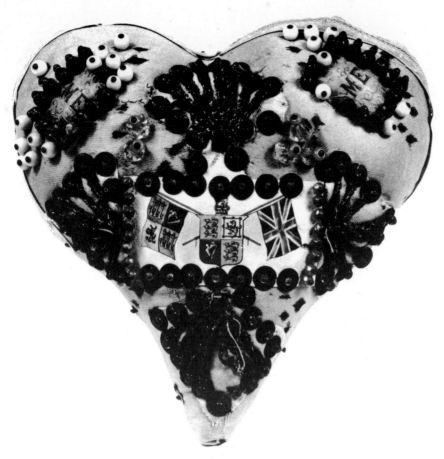

This heart-shaped pin cushion was originally made to attract the evil intended for someone else to the pins, so preserving the life of a relation or loved one. It is thus a useful object and a protective amulet.

A dried sheep's heart, pierced with hawthorn twigs, is used extensively to induce sympathy in a love affair. The figurines are death symbols, and these objects were all found recently, at Castle Rising, Norfolk (above, left).

forthcoming wedding in the house. So does the presence of a butterfly in the house; or two crows circling over it; or three lamps set by chance in a row; or a live coal falling from the fire near someone's feet; or someone stumbling while going upstairs.

As regards the time lapse before marriage: a country girl in Britain can give the first pancake of Shrove Tuesday to the farmyard rooster: the number of hens who come to help him eat it will equal the number of years before she marries. Or, when the first new moon of the New Year appears, she can look at its reflection in a bucket of water, through a silk handkerchief: the number of moons she sees equals the number of years she must wait. (Sometimes impatient maidens interpret these omens in terms of months.) A widespread practice directs the girl to go out of her house early on St Valentine's Day. If the first person she sees is a man, she will be married (not to that man) within three months; if a woman, she must wait at least a year.

If a girl finds a horseshoe, the nails in it will number the years before marriage; so will the eggs in a bird's nest; so, too, will the notes in the first cuckoo's song in spring.

Again, a group of boys and girls, gathered on Hallowe'en, can each tie an apple to a string and whirl it round before a fire. The first apple to fall off signifies who will marry first. He or she whose apple is the last to fall will never marry. And numerous other omens also warn of spinsterhood. Today, people still warn single girls never to take the last piece of bread or cake from the plate. And the old beliefs also say that she must never throw sweepings from the floor towards the sun; nor look under a bed (as old maids are traditionally supposed to do); nor let bread burn; nor keep a crooked pin; nor cut first into fresh butter; nor knock over a chair; nor cut her nails on Sunday; nor walk across a cellar grating; nor harbour a liking for cats (the old maid's traditional companions); nor serve three times as a bridesmaid; nor ever, ever try on someone else's wedding ring.

And omens indicating that a girl will be crossed in love include: kissing over a gate, or when one of the couple is seated, or when the girl is menstruating; putting milk in tea or coffee

44

before sugar; mopping across the cracks
in the floorboards (but some say that
this signifies marriage to a drunkard,
as does spilling flour or wetting the
apron). A girl will also lose her lover if
she loses a hairpin or a garter, or if she
writes a letter to him after dark, or
especially if she gives him a pair of
shoes, which is tantamount to sending
him 'walking away' (compare the old-
shoes tradition at a wedding, mentioned later).

But superstition, always practical,
provides some means of recapturing a
lover should he stray. (These, like love
charms and divinations, are mostly designed for feminine use.) In some cases,
the practice is aimed merely at end-
ing a temporary separation: if her
love is away on a journey, a yearning
maiden can bring him back by pricking
her left-hand 'ring finger' with a needle
and writing in blood, with the same
needle, on a chip of ironwood, her initials and those of the boy. She then
draws three circles around the initials
and buries the chip, and the boy will
be back within three days. Or, more
simply, she can put salt on the fire for
seven consecutive mornings, and the
boy will return.

On the other hand, if the boy is
literally straying, to another girl, magic
again comes to the rescue. First, the
wronged girl must prove to herself
whether or not her love is indeed
unfaithful. A simple test, known
among country folk in the USA,
requires her to light a wooden
match and hold it straight up: if it
curls towards her, or in the direction
of the boy's house, all is well. Otherwise infidelity is certain. Boys, too, can
use this ritual—and can also use the
technique wherein the questioner bends
a mullein stalk towards the lover's
house. If it grows straight again, the
lover is faithful; if it dies, the lover is
false. Twigs of the usual sacred trees
may also be used.

Plants seem to figure large in tests
of fidelity. A country girl will throw a
cocklebur against her skirt, and if it
sticks her boy-friend is faithful. She
may tie knots in a 'love vine', and if
the vine does not die he remains true.
Or she may use one of the many 'he
loves me, he loves me not' counting
games, of which the most familiar today involves the petals of a daisy.
Others employ dandelion fluff, thistle
fluff, and grains on an ear of corn
(maize is most often used, *not* grain).

The binding symbolism of a ring is obvious: in the past, rings were often used to set one's seal on something. The top three show the word 'Love', clasped hands, a wishbone being pulled, and a crowned heart. The large ones are betrothal rings, the smaller are wedding rings.

Confetti – originally rice, to confer the earth's fertility on the bride – is thrown over the couple.

George Brown's daughter (bottom left) rejected superstition when she wore green at her wedding, which took place on a Friday–an unlucky day. She also carried a single rose, and wore no wedding dress.

A blue garter – like Jackie Trent's – is often worn for good luck. Originally, this colour, by association with the Virgin Mary, stood for purity and spiritual strength.

Should he in fact prove untrue, the maiden sets about reclaiming him. Upon going to bed, she can put one shoe across the toe of another, at right angles, thus forming the shape of a 'Tau' cross, and chant:

When I my true love want to see,
I put my shoes in the shape of a T.

Some authorities claim that this is a means of provoking a divinatory dream of the husband-to-be. British girls could choose between two reclaiming rituals using the power of pins and fire. The betrayed girl could insert two pins into a burning candle, through the wick; or she could throw twelve pins into the fire at midnight—but in each case she must say this spell:

'Tis not these pins I wish to burn,
But [name]'s heart I wish to turn.
May he neither sleep nor rest
Till he has granted my request.

If all else fails, a brave girl might approach the darker arts by making an effigy of her lover, binding it with knotted threads of different colours, and carrying it three times around an altar. The 'binding' symbolism is clear: but such techniques, legends say, are used by witches to embroil young people in sinful love, and so must be approached with caution by ordinary folk.

Most of the beliefs and rituals noted so far, in the heady realm of young love, are antiquities of which comparatively few have survived, except in more isolated areas and social backwaters. But such is not the case with the multitude of omens and ritual customs that surrounds the actual sacrament of marriage. In the following account, readers should find many highly familiar ceremonial traditions planted firmly, root and stem, in the earth of superstition. It is as if love, in these free and easy days, can now be allowed to go along without magical aid—but the important rites of marriage still need all the extra insurance, from whatever source, that they can get.

The choice of wedding day itself is of immense importance. Quite apart from reasons of taxation, people today still often avoid marrying in May, but probably without knowing that the month has been considered unlucky for weddings at least since ancient Rome, where May was the month for making offerings to the dead. Any holy day (in

the church calendar) is also to be avoided. June is widely held to be a lucky month, and remains the modern bride's first choice; January, too, has always been thought a suitable time.

In terms of the day of the week, a hoary old rhyme sets out the scale of propriety:

Monday for wealth,
Tuesday for health,
Wednesday the best day of all;
Thursday for losses,
Friday for crosses,
And Saturday no luck at all.

A variation common in New England reverses the result of Monday and Tuesday, but agrees about Saturday. In many parts of northern Europe, though, Thursday is the luckiest day, and Monday—the day of the inconstant moon—the worst. But nearly all places agree that the weather on the wedding day sets the tone for the marital weather: a rainy day means a stormy marriage, while 'happy the bride the sun shines on'. Yet a snowfall on the wedding day is a good omen in parts of the USA. Elsewhere, the eve of the wedding provides omens for the groom:

his happiness depends on the sun shining the day *before* he marries.

The detailed preparations for a wedding require careful attention to omens. For instance, New Englanders say that a bride who makes her own wedding dress will not live to wear it. Nor should she try on her dress before the day, nor, above all, let anyone else try on any of her wedding clothes before her. If a seamstress pricks her finger and allows a drop of blood to fall on the dress, bad luck will follow the bridal pair. But it is good luck to find a spider on a wedding dress, or to find a small accidental tear in the veil.

In many parts of the world girls firmly believe that, for good luck, the entire wedding costume should be brand new—a belief still alieve in the concept of the 'trousseau'. But at the same time it is good luck to have a borrowed veil—especially if it can be borrowed from a woman who has made a demonstrably happy marriage. In this way the very old and still current recipe for bridal wear, 'something old, something new, something borrowed and something blue', can be three-quarters satisfied. As for the something blue, this requirement grows

out of the old stipulations regarding proper colours for bridal gowns. Many rhymes exist containing the rules, of which this one is the briefest:

Blue is true,
Yellow's jealous,
Green's forsaken,
Red is brazen,
White is love
And black is death.

It leaves the bride little choice: and, since white has obvious symbolic connections with purity and virginity, that colour remains the first preference. But a clever girl will increase her luck by means of a touch of blue—a ribbon or a garter—which has since ancient times been the colour of spirituality and constancy.

On the subject of colours, it should be noted that an old Japanese belief forbade anyone, guests and all, to wear purple at a wedding. The reason: purple dye faded faster than other hues, and so would signify the early fading of marital bliss.

Several well-known customs forbid the too-early anticipation of a wedding's result—on the principle that such

47

Horseshoes, bells, doves and shoes – all emblems of good luck – decorated Petula Clark's wedding cake.

Old boots and other objects were often tied to the wedding car. Now cans have super-seded boots, much as confetti has replaced rice.

Lucky cakes, like this one from Pardubice, Czechoslovakia, may be baked in order to ensure that the marriage will be lucky – a reminder of sacrifices to the gods.

anticipation tempted fate. For this reason the bride must not look at herself in a mirror when fully arrayed: so, even today, she will leave her veil off, or her gloves, or leave a few stitches undone in her hem, in order to view herself safely. Nor must she ever see herself in a mirror through her veil. In the same way, she must never see the groom on the appointed day until they are both safely at the altar.

And omens and rituals accompany the couple on their separate ways to the church. The bride must leave her house by the front door (which, in rural communities, is seldom used except on special occasions), and she must step across its threshold with her right foot first. It is a good omen in Britain if she should meet a cat, or a grey horse (or, improbably, an elephant), on the way to the church; it is disastrous if she should meet or even glimpse a funeral. The groom, if at all possible, should drive grey horses to the church; and if they prove recalcitrant it is an evil portent. In modern times this belief has been transferred to motor cars: if the car will not start, or has any trouble *en route*, the omen is bad. Some parts of America advise the bride to

carry salt in her pocket, and the groom to carry a miniature horseshoe in his.

At the church, the bride must enter again with her right foot first, and never by the north door. The groom, of course, will precede her. No mirrors must be allowed in the place where the ceremony will be held; a bat entering the church during the ceremony brings bad luck, as does the ringing of the church bell before the ceremony's conclusion. The couple must never stand with their feet across the cracks in the floorboards (if any); but standing on a white rug is lucky.

Within the ceremony itself, the most important feature for superstition is the ring. Wedding rings go back to pre-history, at least in their older form of *betrothal* rings. The ancient Egyptians placed rings on the fingers of their betrothed, and it is thought that this was partly a symbol of unity and partly a symbol of 'with all my worldly goods I thee endow'. So St Augustine, among others, endorses ring-giving as a symbol of 'earnest-money' (a token of money given to reinforce a pledge). Naturally, voluminous lore has collected around this traditional symbol. Much of it is contradictory: British belief insists that

a woman must never remove her wedding ring, but elsewhere it is permissible (and sometimes considered especially lucky) to borrow a ring for the ceremony. Presumably this belief grew up among the very poor: in fact, in Ireland people used to make money by hiring out rings to those who could not afford their own. Since many other magical rites involve the use of a removed wedding ring, the taboo on removal can be discounted—except, of course, at moments of great travail such as childbirth, when a woman needs her ring to keep away the witches. But a woman must absolutely never *lose* her ring, or her marriage will end in disaster.

In most parts of the world it is a deadly omen if the ring is dropped before being placed on the bride's finger. Yet, oddly, an old French custom *requires* the bride to drop the ring, in order to knock out any devils that may have lodged in it beforehand.

The choice of the third finger, left hand, as the proper place for engagement and wedding rings seems to be less ancient than the rings themselves. Probably it springs from a mistaken belief, in medieval anatomy, that a special nerve or vein travelled straight

from that finger to the heart. In fact, the records of one of Lucrezia Borgia's betrothals, in 1493, state that her ring was placed on the finger 'whose vein leads to the heart'.

When the ring is firmly placed, and all the words spoken, the bridal couple leave the church and are plunged immediately into a welter of rituals, every one designed expressly to ensure that the marriage will prove satisfactorily fertile. For that matter, fertility symbols go with the bride into the church: for instance, orange blossoms are still favoured as part of the bouquet, wreath or head-dress. Before oranges were brought to Britain, myrtle leaves or rosemary served in the same way. (Orange trees, which are evergreen, bloom and bear fruit concurrently, and so are ideal symbols of fecundity.)

The bride's flower girls are descendants of medieval maidens who carried grain in the bridal procession—as a fertility symbol. The gay modern practice of throwing rice (or its imitation, confetti) at the couple is again a fertility ritual. Other places and times used other substances: grain, nuts or fruit, specially-made bread, or small cakes. At some point the cakes became

At the beginning of a marriage among the Araucanian Indians of central Chile, the bridegroom is supposed to seize the woman and ride away with her slung over his horse. If her relatives do not like him, they will stop him. If he succeeds in spite of them, he is deemed to deserve her (far left).

Black cats and toads are well-known as 'familiars', or forms often adopted by witches. Paradoxically a black cat is considered lucky in Britain. Probably the cats' colour and the toads' ugliness are the reasons for their connection with evil. In *Macbeth*, Shakespeare recomended the poisonous entrails of a 'toad that under the cold stone Days and nights has thirty-one, Sweltered venom sleeping got' as the prime requisite for a witch's cauldron.

'The Rape of the Sabine Women', by
Nicholas Poussin.

one large cake, to be cut by the newlyweds and handed round, which lar-
gesse again signifies fecundity. For fertility again, no castrated animal must
provide meat for the wedding feast.
And, in Britain, a nursing mother
should make up the marriage bed, and
perhaps roll a small child across it to
make doubly sure the newlyweds will
have abundant offspring.

The old shoes that so often accompany the bridal couple (thrown, or today tied to their car) are probably
not fertility symbols, though what they
are provides folklorists with a point of
contention. Some say they are an extra
sign of the endowment of the bride
with her husband's worldly goods. But
then why *old* shoes? Others suggest it
continues the ancient tradition of 'marriage by capture', involving battle
(symbolized by thrown shoes). Indeed,
many elements of the wedding seem to
have a flavour of Young Lochinvar or
the Rape of the Sabine Women: especially the hurried flight of the couple
afterwards, and the often secret honeymoon spot. But these parallels can be
stretched too far. More likely (and
with more folklore parallels) is the idea
that giving or even throwing shoes was
a form of sending people on their way
with a 'fare-you-well'.

At least there can be no doubt about
the reason for the bride throwing her
bouquet: whoever catches it, if she is
an unmarried girl, will marry that
year. To obtain a piece of wedding
cake also bodes well for one's marital
hopes—especially if your piece holds
the ring that some bakers still embed

in the cake. But if you get the piece
with a thimble, you will never marry.

Other non-fertility omens, or so they
seem, include the bride removing her
glove (for the joining of hands in the
ceremony) before the groom removes
his. It is bad luck if anything, such as
tableware, is broken during the ceremony or the wedding feast. Conversely,
knots—so often used in magical spells—
are valuable luck-bringers: knots will
be discreetly tied in bridal costumes,
perhaps in ribbons (as the ancient
Chinese used to do). In fact, the joining
of hands is a symbolic knot, often lent
clerical approval when the minister
drops his stole over the clasped hands,
as the Archbishop of Canterbury did at
Princess Margaret's wedding in 1960.
Yet there is no specification for this
action, apparently, in divine service.
Further, it is bad luck to have peacock
feathers in the church during the wedding (because an old belief says this
plumage bears the 'evil eye'). If a doctor witnesses a wedding, it is said, someone present will die within the year.
Wedding gifts are governed by a few
strictures: Kentuckians say one should
never give anything gold, the British
and the Americans avoid giving anything sharp (or the giver's friendship
with the couple will be severed), and
Ozarkians warn a new bride against
beginning married life with a new coffee pot. The groom must carry the
bride across the threshold, possibly another vestige of marriage by capture;
or possibly this reflects the fear of the
bride stumbling on the threshold (for
stumbling is widely held to be a bad

At this Welsh wedding, c. 1860, we see a couple already married being chased by friends and relatives. Formerly, in other countries, an unwelcome groom would have been chased off before the marriage!

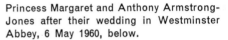

Princess Margaret and Anthony Armstrong-Jones after their wedding in Westminster Abbey, 6 May 1960, below.

The bridesmaids above (left) are 'descendants' of those who carried grain in the wedding procession, to symbolize fertility. To catch the bride's bouquet is a sign that one will be the next to marry.

At this Cumberland wedding real efforts are being made to prevent the couple's getaway. The man must show by his prowess that he deserves the bride. Often the getaway car is 'fixed' too!

52

The bride must be carried over the threshold
– to guard against an unlucky stumble. This
may also derive from the custom of 'marriage by capture', found in many countries.

This wooden figure from Ghana (right) is
carried by pregnant women to make sure
the child has a long and muscular neck –
considered a sign of beauty.

Valentine cards are traditionally received on
the Saint's day; originally it seems to have
been more connected with the pagan worship of Juno than with St Valentine himself.
Birds were popularly supposed to pair off
on this day and lovers could send unsigned
cards in an attempt to influence the course
of events. The custom was temporarily
changed in Victorian days when mothers
often signed cards to their daughters!

omen). Many people believe that the
bride must never wear her wedding
dress again. And, finally, it is said that
the first of the newlyweds to get into
bed, on the wedding night, will die
first.

Some aspects of wedding traditions
seem to have little to do with superstition, but their suggested origins might
be of interest here. The proponents of
the 'marriage by capture' motif find it
again in the bridesmaids and the best
man—representing the two contending
factions, bride's family and groom's
men, who would fight it out while the
abduction took place. (These theorists
also point to the modern 'elopement'
as another survival.) In his less aggress-
ive guise, the 'groom' is thought to be
so called because in some traditions
he is required to wait on the bride,
like a servant, at the feast. And the term
'honeymoon' grows out of an old custom in northern Europe whereby relatives of the couple (and/or the couple
themselves) drank only mead, or similar liquors made from honey, for a
month or 'moon' after the celebrations.

One prominent wedding omen, effective whether occurring before or after the ceremony, must be added—
though it has not survived widely into
modern times owing to the gradual
disappearance of its principal figure.
This is the omen of seeing a chimney-
sweep, preferably one soiled from work,
while the bride is on the way to or
from the church. The sweep's luck-
bringing power is increased if he stops
to offer good wishes, or especially if he
deigns to kiss the bride. Folklorists suggest that the sweep's power may grow
from the ancient association of soot and
ashes with, again, fertility. (Certain
ashes are, of course, valuable as fertil-
izer.) In Continental Europe, and in
Britain, the omen has been considered
powerful enough to warrant *paying*
sweeps to stand by when a wedding was
to pass. And, wherever central heating
has not made these workers redundant,
they will still be so induced. Britons
may remember reports that in 1947,
before his departure for Westminster
Abbey to be married to Princess Elizabeth, Prince Philip came out of
Kensington Palace to shake the hand
of a sweep who was passing by—possibly not by coincidence.

Because in communities where superstition thrives best marital sex is a
private thing, few beliefs concerning
the marriage bed itself, when occupied,

Everybody has somebody! How about you?

Valentine, The reason we go so well together is that we're two of a kind...

The bride sometimes throws her garter to the eager bachelors in the groom's party, who hope that catching it means an early marriage!

birthmark. If a woman is frightened by a hare, the baby will be born with a hare-lip; if by a snake, the baby will have a constricted throat like a serpent. Whatever the object that frightens the mother, the baby will bear a birthmark image of it, like a brand. (In this way, backward communities explain deformed babies.) In fact, if a woman presses her abdomen with her hand, the baby will be marked; if she stretches her arms above her head, the baby will be born with the umbilical cord around its neck.

As might be guessed, folklore also provides ways to predict a child's sex— or even to control it. Dreaming of a juniper tree, in Wales, signifies the birth of a boy. A plentiful crop of nuts, in many British localities, means plenty of boy babies; an unusual number of double nuts within single shells indicates batches of twins.

In France, the hooting of an owl near an expectant mother indicates a girl baby. A boy can be ensured by sticking a knife into the pregnant woman's mattress; a girl, by placing a skillet beneath her bed (the sexual symbolism is obvious). And Ozarkians recommend that the husband sit on his roof, near the chimney, for seven hours in order to produce a son and heir.

Outside the normal course of child-bearing events, magic has answers both for the barren woman and for the woman who would prefer to avoid motherhood. The former, in Britain, was advised to go naked into her garden on Midsummer's Eve and pick the yellow flower called St John's wort. Taking a little milk from a nursing mother is also offered as a curative. So is keeping a nappy (diaper) from another woman's baby, or having a sprig of mistletoe or other powerful plants around the house.

As for avoiding pregnancy, a great number of herbal remedies exist, either as contraceptives or abortifacients, but a few other methods are more explicitly magical. A woman should keep other people's children off her bed. She should ensure that a male guest leaves by the same door through which he entered. And—if it is *more* children she is avoiding—she must never rock an empty cradle, 'or it will soon be filled'. But a woman cannot procure an abortion by breaking on purpose one of the taboos which can cause miscarriage if accidentally broken.

Lord Montague made sure that there was a sweep standing by to give his new wife a kiss for luck.

have been recorded. (Though in many places it was formerly customary, the next day, to display in public the soiled sheets as proof of the bride's innocence.) But once all those fertility rites have taken hold, and the young wife becomes pregnant, the beliefs and rituals bring her out into the public domain again.

Most superstitions concerning pregnancy take the form of 'don'ts', perhaps reflecting the prehistoric and primitive attitude to pregnant women as somehow more open to baleful influences. For instance: she must not step over a grave, or the baby will die. She will miscarry if she climbs over the tailboard of a wagon, or if she stoops under a horse's neck. She must not have her teeth filled (but then modern aentists are wary of treating advanced pregnancies). Above all, she must avoid the multitude of ways in which she can 'mark' her child.

These pernicious fears still hold sway in many parts of the world. Most are obvious forms of sympathetic magic: if the woman craves certain foods and does not satisfy her craving, the baby will bear a mark resembling the food—hence the so-called 'strawberry'

Omens and rituals accompany the mother-to-be to the delivery itself, and try to ensure its relative ease. Before labour, the pregnant woman must never bring a new cradle into the house—an example of the danger in anticipation, which survives today in terms of perambulators. Nor should she make any form of headgear for the baby, or receive one as a gift, or even mention the subject. When labour begins, no doors should be locked in the house, and no knots permitted on her bed-clothing or in her room. A razor-sharp axe under the bed, its blade upwards, assists in a difficult birth—as does salt clenched in the hands of the mother. Old silver coins 'borrowed' from a church can be put into the mattress; an empty hornet's nest in the room is beneficial. Kentuckians recommend tickling the mother's nose with a feather. The mother could also be given a drink part of which has been drunk by another woman; or she could be given (say rural Americans) a potion containing the dried and powdered rattles of a rattlesnake. Church bells ringing during labour are helpful. And many people also play safe by cluttering the room with as many powerful charms and amulets as they can get their hands on. One such, used in the USA, is composed of two hazel twigs (one of many magical trees) crossed on an open Bible and placed beneath the mother's pillow.

When the child is born, midwives check the afterbirth for lumps—for their number indicate how many more children the mother will have. Haemorrhage can be avoided by the voodoo-like practice of burning chicken feathers under the bed. (The area beneath the bed seems widely sacrosanct: many people believe `that it must not be swept during the 'lying-in', or the mother will die.) The afterbirth must then be buried—never burnt or otherwise disposed of—preferably at the chimney-corner of the house.

As for the newborn baby: it will be lucky if born in a covered wagon; or when the mother's head is pointing north; or if it has an extra finger or toe; or if it required a Caesarian operation. If it is born after its father's death, it will have occult powers. It will be unlucky if the moon shines on it, and if it is born with teeth it will either die young or grow up to be a murderer. (In old southern European lore, a baby born with teeth will be a vampire.) If the baby has a prominent blue vein across the bridge of its nose, it will surely die from drowning.

Above all, if part of the amniotic membrane remains clinging to the baby's head, this 'caul' becomes an especially luck-bestowing object. If it is dried and kept safe, the child will be generally lucky, and will never be drowned. In Holland and elsewhere a baby's caul was once thought to endow him (in later life) with psychic powers. And it has a fairly rare quality, among such personal magical objects: if it is sold, its power passes to the buyer. Late in the nineteenth century, advertisements for the sale of cauls appeared frequently in leading British newspapers; and Christina Hole, one of Britain's leading folklorists, records a case known to her of an offer made for a caul in 1954.

In folklore, the time and season of birth naturally affect the child's later chances. (Such beliefs undoubtedly come from a diluted astrology, among people for whom astronomical tables and horoscope interpretations might seem unnecessarily complex.) So a child born on New Year's Day will always

This mask is worn by the Yoruba in Southern Nigeria to promote the fertility of people and crops (far left).

This modern charm is in fact a doll made from a mandrake root, which is usually man-shaped. The charm will bring its owner good luck and a large family.

This advertisement appeared in The Times, 8 May 1848, page 1, at the foot of column 3: 'Child's Caul. Apply at the bar of the Tower Shades, corner of Tower Street. The above article, for which £13 was originally paid, was afloat with its late owner 30 years in all the perils of a seaman's life, and the owner died at last at the place of his birth.'

Below is a tapestry, one of six woven in France for the La Viste family in 1503. It shows the legend that only a virgin holding a mirror can tame the unicorn. The sexual symbolism of the lion, the lance bearing the flag, the crescent-motif, rabbits, holly-berries and oak-leaves suggest that the artist was dealing with the traditions of courtly love.

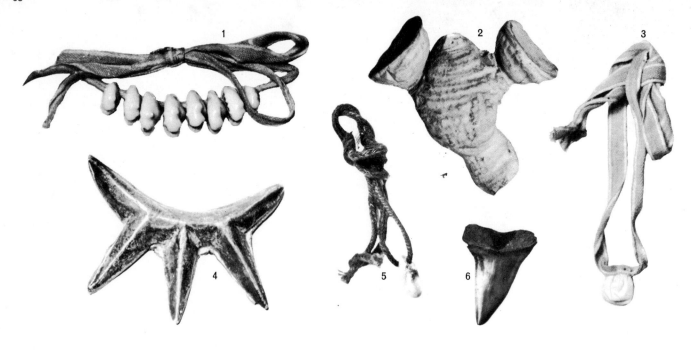

be lucky, while (in the USA) 21 March is the worst possible day. Ozarkians say that children born between 23 June and 23 July will be failures. And May-born babies will always be sickly (compare May weddings). But Christmas Day birth gives a child psychic power. A child born under the new moon will be strong and muscular, but an old belief from Cornwall adds that a child born between the disappearance of the old moon and the first sight of the new will not live past puberty.

A Sicilian belief says that children born under a waning moon will be girls; under a waxing moon, boys. And the moon-controlled tides have their effect: babies born at the ebb will not live long. Similarly, Mr Peggotty in Dickens's *David Copperfield* says that babies simply *cannot* be born until the tide is 'pretty nigh in—not properly born till flood'. The sun plays a part as well: sunrise is a lucky time for birth, but a sunset birth foreshadows laziness. Early-morning babies are often thought to live longer than others.

Almost everywhere there are superstitions regarding the day of birth, usually set out in a rhyme like the following:

Monday's child is fair of face,
Tuesday's child is full of grace,
Wednesday's child is full of woe,
Thursday's child has far to go;

Friday's child is loving and giving,
Saturday's child works hard for a living.
But the child born on the Sabbath Day
Is blithe and bonny, good and gay.

The usual variations occur: for instance, Christina Hole says that in Cornwall and the Scottish Highlands Tuesday's child is 'solemn and sad' while Wednesday's is 'merry and glad'.

At any rate, whether or not the automatic omens are functioning on the child's behalf, the family can take a few precautions. Many Britons put a silver coin into the hand of a newborn (silver invariably has the property of keeping witches off); or the gift might be a little salt. It is wise for someone to carry the newborn three times around the house, to protect him against colic. It is unwise, as regards the child's financial future, to wash his palms for three days after birth. It is generally bad luck to place a newborn on a table, or to pull a dress on it over its head—or, for that matter, to dress it in entirely new clothing. It is beneficial to dress a boy baby (boys are always favourites in the old male-dominated traditions) in blue, the spiritual colour that keeps off evil. (Pink, as a girl's special colour, came much later when the original reason for the boy's blue was mostly forgotten.)

As the days of a newborn's life progress towards baptism and christening, the superstitions mount up—as they always do around a holy time. Prior to the baptism, the new mother must not take the child into any other house, nor herself enter a neighbour's house. (This belief, which keeps mother and child away from possible infection, makes good sense.) Also before baptism, various amulets and charms should be placed in the baby's cradle—such as salt, or those witch-deterrents, garlic and iron—and it is thought unlucky for anyone to pass between the fire and the unbaptized child's cradle.

Baptism and christening, say the old beliefs, must be as soon after birth as possible—to avert diabolic influences, or to drive out those which may already have infested the newborn. Hence a baby's crying at the rite itself is considered a good-luck sign, proving that the devil has been driven out. But the way is opened for evil effects if the minister makes any error in the ceremony. The Scots used to say that if boy and girl babies were brought to the church together for baptism, the boys must always go first, or else the girls would grow up to have beards. Of course the naming ritual is vital, given the power that resides in names: Yugoslavians believed that a boy baby should be given two names, for long life; and it is universally believed that dire luck will follow any change in the name after christening.

Even after the church ceremonies

The amulets on the left prevent bleeding and sore gums. They are: cowrie shells from Russia, 1; an orris root from Poland, 2; a bag of alum from Russia, 3; a charm, a doll's tooth and a fossil shark's tooth, all from Antwerp, 4, 5 and 6.

On the right is a hei tiki from New Zealand. It probably represents the human embryo, and also the spirits of stillborn children. Since they have been cheated of life, these are particularly maleficent and must be placated. This one is unusual in that it has been carved from a skull, and not from the usual greenstone. In a larger form the figure is also associated with Tiki, the Creator in Maori Legend; in both contexts it is probably also a fertility symbol.

Below are amulets for teething children. They are, left to right, a necklace of ivy wood, a piece of orris root from Vienna, a Spanish teething necklace, and a necklet of shells from Jersey.

have conferred some protection, superstitious safeguards can be applied. It is unwise to weigh a baby too soon; it is fatal (to the baby) to take it to a mirror before its first birthday. The baby must be carried upstairs (or generally upwards) before it is taken downstairs, or it will not rise in the world. It must not be tickled under the chin (some say on the feet) or it will stammer. New Englanders used to say that a baby must fall out of bed three times before it is one year old, or it will never know anything. Nor will it if it does not fall downstairs before it is one. Never cut the baby's nails until it is one year old, or it will be a thief: other versions say it will die, as it will if its hair is cut before the twelve-month limit. Never carry a baby in a funeral procession, or it will die. Be careful whom you permit to kiss your baby, for from the first person to do so (other than the mother) the child will draw its temperament. Dress the child in hand-me-downs for luck (a practical belief, which recalls the 'something borrowed' motif in weddings). And never call a baby 'angel', or it will not live long - again exemplifying the fear of tempting fate.

Older babies and young children come in for their share of omens and rituals. An infant's teething will be helped by such charms as nine strands of red silk, with regularly spaced knots, hung round its neck. Kentuckians say

This splendid gold Easter egg was made for the Czar by the renowned Carl Fabergé. Eggs are traditionally associated with spring and rebirth, which suggests that, apart from its doctrinal significance, the Easter festival has much in common with older rites celebrating the death of the winter gods and the upsurge of new life.

Below: the splendid Wilton Diptych in the National Gallery, London, dates from c. 1396 and shows Richard II being presented to the Virgin Mary by St Edmund, King and Martyr, Edward the Confessor and St John the Baptist. The Mother of God has always been clad in blue – hence the special 'spiritual' association of this colour. The ring worn by Richard symbolizes the bonds uniting a monarch and his people. The hart image worn by each person was Richard's personal symbol, reminiscent of the totem beasts of African tribes today.

This print shows May Day being celebrated in eighteenth-century England.

that a child's early teething indicates a new birth coming soon; but many Britons believe that it is a death omen. A child's weaning should begin on church holy days, preferably when the moon is waning.

For good luck, a baby must follow the proper order of things—crawling before walking, walking before talking. And, to assist its talking, some Americans give water in a thimble; while Turks sometimes fed a child the tongues of chattery birds. Yugoslavs say that if a baby's swaddling clothes are made from the shirt-tail of its father, it will talk early and never whimper.

Needless to say, children's illnesses afford much opportunity for folk medicine's extravagances. A drop of mother's milk will cure sore eyes (Christina Hole mentions finding this practice occurring as late as 1949). Saliva is a universal cure-all, for anything from birthmarks to crippled limbs. And Miss Hole, again, tells an astonishing but fairly well authenticated story of how chopped garlic, mixed with lard on brown paper, and fastened to the sufferer's *feet*, proved an effective cure for whooping cough!

From Yugoslavia comes a belief that if a shadow passes over a child's clothes drying on a clothes-line, they must immediately be brought inside or the child will be afflicted with sores. From the USA come beliefs that a male child who persists in wearing a string of beads will be hanged; that a child with a blister on its tongue will be an inveterate liar; that a boy who eats birds' eggs will be sexually abnormal.

Finally, superstition provides various ways to predict a child's future occupation. For instance, a seventh son (where there are no daughters) should be a doctor, while the seventh son of a seventh son *must* be a doctor, for he has near-occult healing powers. And a tenth son will be a preacher. But no divination is so widespread as a simple sympathetic magic wherein the child is surrounded by representative objects. If he first touches, say, a coin, he will be a businessman; if a book, a schoolmaster (but if a Bible, a preacher); if a bottle, a drunkard. An old Chinese version of this practice requires the baby to be placed in a basket with the objects. And if the baby is a girl, her choice reveals her future husband's occupation.

Clearly, with this last belief, the cycle has begun again. For girls, it seems, love divination begins in the cradle. And of course there must come a point in a child's life when he can no longer be governed by the specialized magic that operates on children— when he becomes a full member of the community and begins to comport himself according to its general superstitious rules.

COMMON FEARS

Some superstitious beliefs grow out of a positive hope or desire, such as a general hope for good fortune, success, prosperity, or a particularized hope of achieving some specific goal. But a far larger proportion arise from negative emotions, principally fear. Even the positive beliefs may have their negative side: the girl who performs rituals to realize her hopes of marrying will at the same time be motivated by a fear of remaining an old maid; or a sportsman may fear a loss of skill.

The most powerful fears—and the most abundant store of compensating superstitions—lie in the morbid and gloomy areas of illness and death. In the primitive past such matters were shrouded in great mystery, and ascribed to supernatural causes. Then special magic was hastily worked out to hold these causes at bay. And much of this magic has stayed very much alive (though perhaps mostly in cultural backwaters) as a kind of underground knowledge, during the growth of modern scientific medicine.

Not that this underground knowledge, all the old wives' cures of folk medicine, has been based solely on sorcery. Often the doctoring employed substances or methods with some recognizable medical legitimacy. Some of these will be mentioned later, but three special cases can be described here.

The Indians of Peru knew that an extract from the bark of the cinchona tree would reduce a fever; thanks to them, seventeenth-century Europe acquired quinine from the bark, to cure malaria. A substance made from the leaves of the foxglove plant, folk medicine says, is useful for heart ailments: modern medicine uses it too, and calls it digitalis. And in 1966 doctors engaged in cancer research at the University of Wisconsin found a new avenue opening up when they discovered that an extract of woody nightshade had a marked healing effect on cancer in mice. They are presumably continuing their work, unabashed by the fact that in folk medicine nightshade has been used as a cure for tumourous growths since at least the second century AD.

So folk medicine has one or two of its feet on the ground, and the herbalist muttering over his roots and leaves is not altogether a comic figure. Further to this point: no one would deny that a hot drink of any sort will soothe the symptoms of a sore throat or cold; no one would deny that poultices can be useful for many skin disorders. Does it really matter if the hot drink has been made by boiling pine needles, or the poultices from fresh cow-dung?

Yet magic, as will be seen, remains hovering on the fringe of many such cures. Where, for instance, magic moves in to *dominate* the scene is in the case of folklore's preventives—the techniques of forfending illness.

Frequently the prevention is accomplished by means of amulets, lucky charms aimed at specific diseases. Perhaps they will be decorative necklaces: gold beads worn round the neck prevent, and/or cure, a host of ailments including a sore throat and goitre, quinsy and scrofula. Green beads prevent the disease called erysipelas, or St Anthony's Fire, once widespread before antisepsis conquered it. It is widely believed that the general luckiness of a horseshoe nail, carried in the pocket, can be focussed on preventing rheumatism; which disease can also be avoided by carrying a horse chestnut, or alum, or the ashes of a burnt toad, or brimstone, or the knucklebone of a sheep, or a new potato. Some of these ideas seem to be intended as means of *diverting* the disease: perhaps the sheep-bone is supposed to become rheumatical instead of the carrier's joints; and the potato apparently should be carried until it is black and rock-hard, by which time it presumably has 'absorbed' the illness. Charms absorb evil in the same way.

Some preventives strike the observer as incredibly primitive, direct from the Stone Age. An old Kentucky belief states that the rattles from a rattlesnake, worn in the hair, prevent headache. A widespread American belief says that brass rings or earrings prevent cramp (and, sometimes, rheumatism), while in certain backwoods areas copper wire twined round an arm or leg has been used to protect the wearer against venereal disease. In many parts of the world mothers will put a live fish (or the head of a live fish) into a child's mouth for a moment, to save him from whooping cough. Sulphur and brimstone are made to be generally useful: some American mothers will still administer sulphur and molasses to their children, in spring, as an all-round disease repellent; brimstone carried in the pocket keeps off scarlet fever and scrofula. Both substances, so

Silver coins stop this corpse 'looking for someone to join him'.

A Zulu witch-doctor blows into a patient's ear through a cow-horn to cure deafness. It is actually the breath which is believed to heal: in primitive medicine, spittle, blood, breath and other excretions all have a part to play because they were once connected with the body, and hence with its spirit.

A woodcut of *Digitalis Purpurea* (the fox-glove) from an old Herbal of 1540. It contains the drug digitalis, used in the treatment of some heart diseases. Many folk cures contain important elements of fact: mouldy bread, for instance, was shown to contain penicillin; soldiers had used it on wounds for centuries.

Digitalis purpurea.

Brauner Fingerhut.

often associated with folklore ideas of hell, are thus being turned to good purpose in holding off the demonic visitations of disease—fighting, as it were, fire with fire.

New England lore states that silver (perhaps a coin on a string) worn round the neck holds off illness in general—because of the old belief that evil in all forms shies away from that metal. Many people believe that carrying an onion maintains health, especially in relation to colds—and, as a parallel, mothers once sewed bags of camphor or the equally strong-smelling asafoetida inside their children's clothing. Here the principle seems to be that a powerful odour is enough to hold evil at bay—rather in the way that garlic imposes a barrier to vampires.

Treatment of wounds, to prevent festering, often requires ritual action that would not seem out of place in the repertoire of a witchdoctor. Traditional lore in Europe and America demands that if you injure yourself with a knife, axe, or similar implement you must treat the *implement*. In this form of sympathetic magic, little attention is paid to the wound: anything on the cutting edge or point that might

cause a wound to fester must be removed, or otherwise counteracted—and thus any infection in the wound will be sympathetically overcome. An offending knife must be plunged into the earth; the curative powers of Mother Earth will be transferred from weapon to injury. Or the injurious object should be cleaned and highly polished, and kept free from rust and stains until the wound heals. Often people will continue to polish the object long after the healing is complete—even for years—believing that otherwise the wound would re-open. (If the wound does fester, instead of healing, then something went wrong with the cleaning process.) Sometimes special salves or ointments are made up for the purpose of tending the implement when someone has hurt himself. Christina Hole provides a gruesome recipe for such an ointment, which includes stale grease from a boar, powdered bloodstones, powdered worms, and moss from a disinterred human skull. To prevent tetanus when one has stepped on a rusty nail, one must clean the nail, grease it with some ointment, and hang it in the chimney. Lacking the ointment, one should clean it somehow as with

the knife or axe and perhaps drive the nail into some hard wood that has a magical association.

Clearly, in the realm of prevention, magic is all, and folk *medicine* gets hardly a look in. It is as if disease must be wholly a baleful, evil force when viewed in the abstract, avoidable only through charms and rituals. When it actually strikes, when it appears in a human body, it becomes apparent and *physical* enough to be treated by means of actual medicaments and herbal remedies.

Some of these, as mentioned before, may seem more or less reasonable in principle—though scarcely appealing, or acceptable to modern hygienic medical practice. Ear-ache, in the American backwoods, has been treated by pouring in skunk oil (made from boiling the fat of skunks). And modern doctors accept that warm oil put into the ear does relieve the pain. They might jib, however, at the use of warm water through which tobacco smoke has been bubbled; or the fresh urine of mules; or a concoction made by boiling the seeds of an ash tree in the patient's own urine. (There are magical elements in this last: urine, like

Two mole's feet in a satchel form a magical protection against rheumatism (above, left).

This Egyptian glass amulet is thought to have been worn for protection from the evil eye, which was long thought to be responsible for disease and misfortune.

Cinchona Officinalis – Jesuit's bark, from which we eventually derived quinine – was known by Central American Indians for its curative powers.

These silver coins, or 'touch-pieces', were thought to convey the King's power over scrofula to their owners, once the King had touched them. One of the last people to receive one (the coin on the left) was Dr Johnson, as a child in Queen Anne's reign.

Charles II touching subjects to heal them of scrofula, or 'King's Evil', as it was known. This was one of the many ailments which used to be held to be cured by this Royal touch, a manifestation of the Divine Right of Kings.

These charms to ward off nightmares come from London, and date from the nineteenth century. They are horseshoes, and a necklace of stones.

This amulet above contains the remains of a dead man, and is worn by a relative during mourning. It is thought to be capable of stopping pain and disease if applied to the affected part.

other excreta of the human body, has much magical virtue; and the ash tree is sacred and magical in the mythologies of Greece, Rome, Scandinavia and ancient Britain.)

A fairly legitimate cure for sores on the skin, in rural America, employs poultices made by crushing and boiling a plant called sheep sorrel—which apparently contains oxalic acid, and so will do some good. In Britain, the juice of the leek is used for the same purposes, and is also acknowledged to have some valid medicinal properties.

In the same way, one can accept that goose grease or rattlesnake oil might well soothe aching backs. but with the qualification that the massage implicit in the application of any liniment helps as much as the ingredients. Similarly, various repulsively bitter substances, often made from the bark of trees, can act as purgatives, but perhaps only because the body wants to get rid of the stuff.

Other cures and treatments within the herbalist's armoury put a greater strain on our credulity. Odd poultices may be useful for certain ailments, but perhaps not a chicken-dung-and-lard poultice for pneumonia, a tobacco poultice for bullet wounds, or the cow-dung poultice mentioned earlier as applied to cancer. So, too, one can doubt that mare's milk has much effect on whooping cough, or milk from a dish at which a fox has previously drunk. Equally doubtful are prescriptions of chewing turnip root for a fever, drinking tea made from plantain leaves for measles, or eating hazel nuts for sores in the mouth. In these examples as in the literally innumerable herbal remedies known round the world, magic is not far away. In fact, the mixture seems to be half magic and half folklore medicament. In the whoop-ing cough cure, the fox brings to the remedy the supernatural power with which it is invested in the lore of every European country where the animal is found. (Witches were believed often to assume the shapes of foxes, when they were not changing into cats, toads or spiders.) As for the mouth sores, hazel nuts and their tree are sacred in the ancient Celtic religion of which many fragments still thrive in Europe and Britain.

As further examples, it appears that pills made from rolled spiders' webs have been used to cure asthma, and pills made by rolling fishworms in lard and cooking them are administered for jaundice. Drinks made from the leaves of violets (which function in many divination rituals) are said to cure fevers, jaundice and pleurisy, and to relieve the pains of cancer. Nettle seeds are prescribed for someone bitten by a rabid dog. A pinch of gunpowder in warm water has been offered as a cure for diphtheria. And sexual debility is supposedly overcome by the sufferer's eating the fat from rabbits' kidneys. (The sympathetic magic in the last item is surely obvious.)

A strong element of magical ritual often exists in the preparation of herbal cures—usually relating to the choice of time for the gathering or mixing of ingredients. Sometimes the time is appointed by astrological means—since in astrology the various parts of the body, and their afflictions, have direct planetary or zodiacal connections. So, too, the moon plays an important part in folk-medicine ritual. An old American cure for fevers demands that the sufferer be rubbed with oil from a turtle killed at the waning of the moon—symbolizing the waning of the fever. The herb vervain, believed medicinally

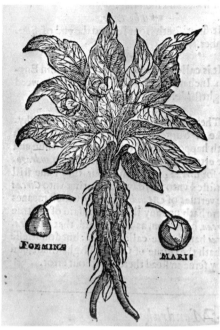

Shown here (at top left) are amulets worn against cramp: an eelskin from Carlisle, a hare's foot from Sussex and two London cockspurs.

Mandragora, or mandrake root, (above) is credited with many powers, perhaps because its shape resembles that of the human body. It was once thought to shriek when pulled from the ground.

In Finland, spring water is gathered by a Tietäjä, or wizard, for healing the sick. It must be paid for with 'silver taken from a corpse'.

In the Tarot pack – often used for fortune-telling – Death is nameless.

powerful at least since Druidical times, must be gathered during specified phases of the moon, always with the speaking of secret incantations. Other cures relate to times of the year: the plant St John's wort, used in Britain to cure nervous disorders, must be gathered on Midsummer's Eve—which is St John's Eve. Bread baked on Good Friday, or Christmas Day, has been thought to cure dysentery and diarrhœa. Chewing the first fern to be seen in spring is said to relieve toothache.

The connection of ritual and the gathering process reaches something of an extreme in one saying of old American herbalism. It is said that if the bark of the peach tree is scraped off downwards, it will brew up into a powerful purgative; if scraped upwards, it becomes an equally powerfull *anti-emetic* that stops all vomiting and diarrhœa. But the magical mandrake root takes the honours in herbal extremism, and has done so (as the Book of Genesis reveals) since Biblical times. Legend says that it cannot be gathered by humans, for when it is uprooted it emits an agonized shriek that causes instant madness or death to the hearer. So the herbalist tied a dog to the plant, left some meat just out of the dog's reach, and hastily retired. The dog then pulled up the plant, and presummably died or went mad—or perhaps not, not being human. The forked root of the mandrake, resembling the human legs and crotch, then went into cures for sterility and insomnia, and into aphrodisiacs and purgatives.

Less extreme but still magical ele-ments occur in some apparently fairly practical old wives' cures which have little to do with herbalism. New England superstition recommends treating a sore throat by tying round the neck, overnight, a stocking worn by the sufferer that day. Presumably the warmth will do some good, but the stocking is also thought to shift the 'bad blood', sympathetically, down into the feet, in the same way that rubbing the feet with goose grease (another old American cure) is thought to cure colds in the head. A red flannel around the neck also helps a sore throat: the flannel is practical treatment, but its prescribed colour is magical. (Red is the colour of healing, probably from association with that old cure-all of the past, blood-letting. The founders of the International Red Cross were thus doubly knowledgeable in their choice of symbol.) The widely familiar use of cobwebs to stop bleeding has a practical side, for the webs (however unhygienic) do help the coagulating process, just as surgical gauze does. But the effect is assisted by the superstitious belief in spiders as harbingers of good luck.

In America the old wives relieve the pain of burns with a mixture of elder bark and goose grease; in England, elder bark and butter are used for the same object. The grease, keeping the burn air-proof, does stop the pain; but the presence of the elder, one of the favourite woods in the spells of sorcery, has only a magical value. An application of dew is said in Britain to help clear up skin troubles: perhaps the

At one time, moles were thought, by their position on the body, to show which planets exerted influence over the personality. On the face, the most obvious indicator, the planets are sketched in detail.

mere act of washing, in a clear liquid, might be beneficial in some cases; but the prescription of dew recalls its ancient prominence in mythology and magical lore.

Folk medicine contains an enormous variety of these borderline cures, half practical, half magical, as it does of the wholly practical (speaking in terms of folklore) herbal remedies. But even this large array of backwoods doctoring is overshadowed by the immense quantity of *entirely* magical remedies in which so much of the familiar apparatus of ritual, charm and incantation is brought to bear. Within this area, perhaps no single ailment receives more attention than that more or less harmless, if unsightly, tumour called the wart.

It seems likely that the full-scale war on warts grew out of the superstitious association of these growths with the Adversary himself. Witchhunters of the fifteenth and sixteenth centuries believed that the Devil left his mark, as proof of guilt. Also, the witchhunters

believed that practising witches possessed other blemishes, the 'witches' marks'—raised protuberances through which the familiars (or imps) fed by sucking the witches' blood. Warts qualify in these terms too. So it is no wonder that superstitious men and women, even today, vaguely connect warts with evil and seek to get rid of them by fighting the supernatural with the supernatural. (Incidentally, the widespread belief that handling toads will somehow cause warts may grow, not only from the creature's own warty appearance, but from its association with witches and their familiars, who were often supposed to assume toad form.) To rid yourself of warts, you can bathe the warts in stump water (sometimes at midnight, or under a full moon) or in the blood of, variously, a cat, pig, mole, mouse or eel. With reference to the toad motif, rural English lore states that you may cure your warts by carrying a live toad in a bag around your neck, until the animal dies; or by carrying a toad's leg. You

may cut your warts off with a silk thread (or a horse hair) and they will not grow again. You may smother a mole and hold the body above your head for a moment: somehow this cruelty drives off the warts. If you are desperate you can get up at midnight and make faces at yourself in the mirror (to frighten off the evil within you?) for three successive nights. British lore suggests blowing on the warts nine times when the moon is full; American lore recommends rubbing the warts three times, while gazing at the new moon and intoning 'You grow and you go', whereupon the warts should wane as the moon waxes.

Many wart cures involve the principle of magical transference, i.e. the sufferer ritually passes the warts on to someone or something else. Rub the warts with an apple and bury it; as it decays the warts will fade. Beans can also be used, one for each wart. Southern Americans sometimes tie knots in string, one knot per wart, and bury the string to decay. In Britain, notches

In this West African ritual, the sickness has been transferred to two fowls and the remains are being brushed away. The birds will then be sacrificed to Elegba, protector of families.

Left: this Greek rhizotomist, or herbalist, figures in a seventh-century manuscript. As a form of healing, herbalism is still widely practised.

can be cut in an elder stick which is then buried. Similarly the wart can be rubbed with a pod containing nine peas, which is then thrown away with the admonition, 'Wart, wart, dry away'. In the USA the wart should be rubbed with *stolen* bacon, which is then buried; another version of this belief uses a stolen dishcloth.

You may prick your warts each with an individual pin which has previously been jabbed into an ash tree, then return the pins to the tree. Or, Ozarkians say, you should prick your warts with pins, blindfold yourself, and thrust the pins into the ground. (In each case the pins must never afterwards be disturbed.) Elsewhere in North America people say that you should draw a knife blade flat across the warts and then across the bark of an apple tree. You can also rub the warts with a pebble, while walking nine steps backwards, then throw the pebble away without looking. In some formulas, it is thrown over the left shoulder

This is a Japanese charm for curing small-pox and other skin diseases. The patient puts inside a figure of himself and a bowl of rice, and prays on the hill until his disease is cured.

into a running (magical) stream or river.

Animals can become recipients in many ways, some quite cruel. In British lore, you can rub a live frog over your warts and impale it on a thorn tree to die; another version uses a black snail, which dies the same way. Or you can make your warts bleed, put a drop of blood from each wart on a grain of corn, and feed the corn to a red rooster or a gander. Or take a grain of corn for each wart and hide the corn under a thin stone in a roadway near a crossroads. Whoever disturbs the stone—most likely an animal or a bird—will 'take' the warts.

Also, you may pass them to other people. A common belief requires a friend's help: he offers to 'buy' your warts for a token sum of money; they will leave you without afflicting him. In other rituals, an unwilling recipient is afflicted. Put blood from your warts onto a coin and throw it away; the finder gets your warts. Or rub the warts with a pebble, write an enemy's

name on a scrap of paper, wrap the pebble in the paper and throw the whole thing away—to give your warts to the enemy.

Many of these cures seem outlandish (though most are still flourishing) because of the hopeful but apparently indiscriminate use of magical motifs. From examples in the last two paragraphs alone, the black snail, red rooster, stones, pebbles, metal coins, blood, all have their associations with supernatural power. Similar elements and motifs appear in some remarkable rituals for curing diseases.

Here, too, the principle of transference can be found. An old American cure for chills and fever requires the sufferer to drive, in utmost secrecy, a hickory peg into the ground, then to visit it (always secretly) on twelve successive days, and each time to pull it up, blow seven times into the hole and replace it. Thus he is putting the disease into the wood and earth by means of his breath. A cure for asthma in-

This spirit-scaring effigy (below) from the Indian Ocean is used to cure diseases, which are often thought to be caused by evil spirits.

Goya knew his folk medicine well, as this etching by him shows: 'The teeth of a dead man are indispensible for spell-binding; without this ingredient, nothing succeeds'.

volves the patient boring a hole in a black oak tree at head height, putting in a lock of his hair (through which the disease is transferred) and driving in a peg to hold the hair within the tree. Kentuckians cure colds by placing a hair or nail clipping into a hollow tree. To cure a toothache, pick the tooth with a poplar splinter until it bleeds, then wrap the splinter in yarn and have it buried by another person.

Toothache can also be cured by carrying—in the teeth—the skull or jawbone of a horse as far as is possible, in complete secrecy. Backache is curable if a seventh child can be induced to walk up and down your back seven times. Boils can be cured by rubbing a greasy string on a rusty nail, throwing the nail away, hanging the string inside the door and touching the boil to it several times a day. Also, for boils, draw a circle around the infected spot with the burnt end of a stick, and mark a cross in the centre. The head of a buzzard tied round the neck will cure

This mask is used by the all-female Bundu cult of Sierra Leone to encourage beauty in the babies of its members. Beauty is here stylised in braided hair and a tall, many-ringed neck.

Opposite: this Victorian Valentine shows doves and wild roses, which have always been symbols of love.

'The Dance of Death': a familiar presentation in Mediaeval European art, it shows death pursuing his victims. Its origin was the pulpit, and it was a good example of the way in which the Church played on superstition and fear of the Plague to strengthen its following. Note, incidentally, the ravens – traditionally birds of ill-omen, and the fact that this is taking place at a crossroads – always associated with evil spirits.

Even the most serious diseases are thought to succumb to magic. A cancer cure involves drying and powdering horse 'spurs' (callouses from the inside of the horse's leg) and drinking the powder in ale. And tumours generally can be cured by a ritual wherein a vervain root is cut in half, one half worn round the sufferer's neck and the other dried over a fire. As the root dries the tumour is supposed to wither away. Rheumatism can be overcome (in America) by wearing rattlesnake skin round the affected part, or rubbing it with the yellow ('gold') meat of a turtle.

A mythical stone from the body of a swallow, if taken from the bird under the August full moon, cures epilepsy. A plaster for the chest made from clay taken from the threshold cures influenza. A sheep's lung attached to the sufferer's feet cures pneumonia. And, for tuberculosis, one may merely walk round a sheep-fold early in the morning and then several more times during the day; or eat butter from the milk of cows that have grazed in a churchyard (i.e. a cemetery); or, in the USA, it is enough to wear a

a headache, and the stomach of a cormorant tied at the waist will relieve stomach pains.

Even the most serious diseases are thought to succumb to magic. A cancer cure involves drying and powdering horse 'spurs' (callouses from the inside of the horse's leg) and drinking the powder in ale. And tumours generally can be cured by a ritual wherein a vervain root is cut in half, one half worn round the sufferer's neck and the other dried over a fire. As the root dries the tumour is supposed to wither away. Rheumatism can be overcome (in America) by wearing rattlesnake skin round the affected part, or rubbing it with the yellow ('gold') meat of a turtle.

A mythical stone from the body of a swallow, if taken from the bird under the August full moon, cures epilepsy. A plaster for the chest made from clay taken from the threshold cures influenza. A sheep's lung attached to the sufferer's feet cures pneumonia. And, for tuberculosis, one may merely walk round a sheep-fold early in the morning and then several more times during the day; or eat butter from the milk of cows that have grazed in a churchyard (i.e. a cemetery); or, in the USA, it is enough to wear a

wristband made of rattlesnake skin.

Folk medicine has its share of queer curative incantations. Hiccoughs can be cured, according to American belief, by placing the thumb against the lower lip (with fingers under the chin) and saying nine times, 'hiccup, hiccup, over my thumb'. If this fails, then say all in one breath the following obscurely morbid lines:

There was an old woman who lived all alone
And she was made of skin and bone.
One day she went to the church to pray,
And on the ground a man there lay,
And from his head unto his feet
The worms crawled in, the worms crawled out.

A cure for ringworm requires you to spit on your index finger and move it in circles on the bottom of a used cooking pot, chanting:

Ringworm round,
ringworm red,
ringworm die
to make (name) glad.

For burns, the following lines are effective:

Two little angels come from heaven,
One brought fire, the other brought frost.
Go out fire, come in frost.

Many backwoods healers have a power to stop bleeding, usually by walking towards the east and speaking a Biblical verse, Ezekiel 6 : 16, which reads in part: 'And when I passed by thee, and saw thee polluted in thine own blood, I said unto thee when thou wast in thy blood, Live'. At this point the healer speaks the sufferer's name, and the bleeding should stop.

Perhaps no folk cures remain so startling to modern minds as those which directly involve some aspect of death, because of the immense magical power, in primitive minds, that accrues to the dead and anything associated with them. So dirt from a new grave clears up warts. Goitre is curable by an application of dew gathered in May, before sunrise, from a young man's grave—gathered by passing the hand three times over the grave from its head to its foot. In Britain, mould from a grave, heated, will cure a stitch—providing the mould is returned to the grave before sunset. In the Ozarks, sores, syphilis and cancer could all be cured by an application of powder made by grinding the bones of a long-dead corpse.

The touch of the dead is extremely powerful, in curative superstition, and all over the world diseases, especially of the skin, are treated by this method. In many cases the cure is more effective if the dead person died violently—preferably by hanging. The touch of such a corpse's hand is said to cure everything from wens and warts to sterility and cancer. In the Middle Ages, in Europe, the blood from a hanged man was thought to be a certain cure for leprosy. Also in Europe, a strand from the hangman's rope, worn inside the hat, cured a headache; in Britain, a similar strand worn round the neck cured epilepsy.

The dark supernatural mysteries that surround death itself—at the point, one might say, when folk medicine fails—produce a rich variety of superstitions. They fall into two general classes: the omens of impending death, and the magical rituals with which people deal with the dead. Many of the former still spark that 'half-belief' in modern minds; and some of the latter have become so familiar a part of our funerary ceremonies that their magical origin has been largely forgotten.

First, the omens. Many of these warnings simply grow out of association with dark, gloomy, lugubrious matters; others employ familiar magical motifs, while a few seem to have no overt connection whatsoever with morbidity. In the case of individual omens, a man knows he is to die if he sees a star fall, or a flower blooming out of season. Death is approaching him if he hears a ringing in his ears; if a black beetle runs over his shoe; if he sees a butterfly at night; if he dreams of cats (in Brittany, hares), or sees two cats fighting; if he hears a rooster crow at midnight; if a cow lows three times in his face; if he is looking at the ground when he hears the first cuckoo of spring (in Germany, if he is looking northwards); if crows or magpies flutter round him; if a footprint fitting his foot appears in the fireplace ashes on St Mark's Eve (24 April); if, as is believed in parts of France, an inexplicable shiver comes over him. Personal omens using direct death motifs include beliefs that a man will die if he is cut by a razor that has shaved a corpse; if he sees his reflection in the glass of a hearse, or sees a corpse's reflection in a mirror; if a single ray of sunlight falls on him at a funeral, or if he stumbles near the open grave at a funeral; if his is the last name to be spoken by a dying man.

A person can inadvertently bring about his death by committing various more or less innocent but magical acts. For instance, by transplanting cedar or willow trees; by burning elder wood, or wood of a tree struck by lightning, or the Christmas holly decoration when still green; by cutting down a juniper tree; by planting lily of the valley in his garden. If three people make a bed together, or are reflected together in a mirror, one of them will shortly die. If you mend your clothes while wearing them, the act presages your death. So does lying on a table, or building onto your house. Above all, you will shortly die if you play funerals, or wear mourning unnecessarily, or carry a spade over your shoulder through the house, or pass in front of the casket during a funeral procession, or point at such a procession.

Flowering blackthorn – thought to have provided the Crown of Thorns – is still held to be an unlucky thing to have inside the house.

You can inadvertently cause the death of others through certain actions (which presumably do not work if they are murderously premeditated). If you bring a flowering blackthorn branch indoors (or white lilac, or flowering hawthorn), someone therein will die. If you sing at the table, a friend or relative will die; if a housewife washes clothes on Good Friday, or blankets anytime in May, or sweeps the house on Good Friday or New Year's Day, or after dark, a relative will die. The same will happen if you leave a candle burning in an empty room, or let a lamp burn dry. A death will occur in the family of one who comes late to a funeral, or who is the first to turn away from the graveside at a funeral. And a sick person will die if you move him to a different bed, or shave him in bed, or sweep under his bed. (Incidentally, superstition says that sick people are most likely to die at four a.m., or during rain, or at the ebb tide.)

Omens warning of an unspecified death in the house or the family are legion in folklore. Most of us are familiar with the belief that a dog howling near a house foretells the death of an occupant. Other animal beliefs usually involve especially nocturnal creatures, or those of funereal aspect. So death will come to a house if a cat licks the door; if a bat flies three times round the house; if a crow flies three times over it, or flutters at the window, or if a crow's call is heard near the house, or if four crows fly over; if a raven croaks nearby, or a weasel cries, or an owl hoots. Death omens borne by birds are doubly fearsome if the bird actually enters the house—and this applies to pigeons, swallows and sparrows as well as to the more gloomy birds. In parts of the USA there is a counter-charm to the owl omens. If the bird hoots, salt can be thrown into the fire. If the omen occurs with a sick person in the house, the owl must be caught, killed, and its body placed on the invalid's chest.

Further animal omens include the fear of a live adder on the doorstep; a cow lowing at midnight, or cattle breaking into the garden; a white pigeon on the chimney (the symbol of peace, used in a different sense); a hen trying to crow, or all the chickens taking to their roosts in the forenoon; two white horses pulling a hearse; a black cat crossing in front of a funeral procession. Some of these may derive from the old folk belief that animals can sense the approach of death, but of course most of these animals are closely associated with the supernatural in other areas as well.

Finally, among some miscellaneous death omens, another old favourite should be mentioned: the tolling of a bell when no one has touched it. Similarly inexplicable occurrences presaging death include a window blind falling without being touched, or a picture falling from its nail. (These happenings have something of the poltergeist about them, and superstitious people will immediately fear the worst.) If double-yolk eggs are laid by one's hens; if scissors are dropped and fall point downwards; if cracks appear on the top of a freshly baked loaf of bread; if a candle burns blue; if, after apple-picking, one apple remains on a tree till spring; if bay trees in a garden die; if a white bean plant appears in a bean patch; in all these cases death is said to follow along. If a corpse is carried from one house to another, death will occur in the second house. If rain falls at a burial, it foretells another

At Singapore funerals, umbrellas and the sacred colours blue and yellow are used to ward off evil spirits.

Church bells have a dual rôle, and are associated with death and mourning as well as weddings.

death in the bereaved family, although this omen, in some parts of the world, bodes well for the departed.

When death occurs—which perhaps is to say when an omen is fulfilled— several rules and rituals come immediately into play. The doors and windows of a room in which someone has died should be opened, to speed the departing spirit. In some regions of the USA, the family will place a plate of salt in the room, to overcome any evil powers that might be lurking within. Mirrors must be covered, both to prevent the living from seeing the corpse reflected in them (see the death omen above) but also to prevent the newly freed soul from being trapped there. For the latter reason, too, all knots must be untied in the death-room. The coffin must be taken into the room where the corpse lies; in any other room, it would mean the death of the occupant. A church bell, the 'passing bell', should be tolled as a way of calling for the prayers of the locality, and also as a means of driving away any evil spirits that might have gathered for the occasion. All animals must be kept out of the corpse room, especially cats and dogs, for if one of these should jump over the body, or later over the coffin, the omen is disastrous and the animal must immediately be killed to avert bad luck.

The dead must never be left alone, folk tradition says, nor should they lie in a locked room or in darkness. Candles are usually lit to fulfil the last requirement, keeping evil forces from the body. The famous Irish tradition of the 'wake' grew out of this belief in keeping the corpse company—and staying awake while doing so. All over the world the belief can still be found that clocks should be stopped as near to the moment of death as possible. This ritual may be a gesture to honour the dead, for traditionally the clock should stop of itself, especially if it is the head of the family who has died. If the clock has not acted suitably (as in the well-known song where 'the clock stopped, never to go again, when the old man died'), it must be made to do so.

In many rural areas some member of the family must formally tell the cattle of their owner's death, or the animals will pine and die. Rooks nesting nearby should also be informed. Most importantly, any bees kept by the deceased must be told, preferably by the

In 1620 the wrath of God was manifested by a vision of armed men and a rain of blood falling on the tomb of Mahomet (left).

In Hanoi, white is the colour used for funerals, as death is seen as a joyful occasion for the departed (right).

These sugar skulls are distributed on the Feast of the Dead (November 2) in Mexico. Each one bears the name of the receiver to familiarize him with the idea of death. This is the survival of a pre-Christian rite in Catholic surroundings, and an example of the diverse elements contained in Christianity (left).

Black has always been the colour of death in the West, since death is for us a matter of mourning and sorrow. Notice the canopy-like construction of the hearse, which is a survival of much older trappings. Originally, a harrow was used as an elementary chandelier, and supported over the coffin on four poles (right).

This Cambodian Buddhist coffin is about to be burnt: this ritual seems to have pre-Buddhist origins.

At another stage in the funeral shown opposite the priest will pour water into the teapot seen above, to symbolize the way in which good deeds performed by the living relatives and friends of the deceased may 'flow into' the dead person.

This Nigerian figure above was one of those carved on the death of an important man or woman, and was placed by the skull for a day to acquire some of that person's life-force.

The cars in this Chinese funeral-procession in San Francisco, California, are showing their lights: originally this was done to scare away evil spirits (above, right).

These two people sleeping under a yew tree would surely die, according to beliefs current in 1491, when this woodcut (right) was made. Perhaps the tree's connection with graveyards and its poisonous qualities helped to give the yew tree this reputation.

This woodcut shows the burial customs of a tribe in Central America: the grave is being filled with food and tools for the life beyond (top far right).

Far right: this Egyptian tomb painting shows food assembled to accompany the dead man.

eldest son, who should knock three times on the hives and say, 'The master is dead'. Otherwise the bees, traditionally bearers of luck and good magic, will leave and take their good luck (not to mention their honey) elsewhere. In some parts of Britain, after a death, bits of black crêpe or mourning cloth are tied to favourite plants in the deceased's garden, to prevent them from pining away.

The western tradition that mourners should wear sombre clothing after a death in the family is thought, today, to be merely a way of showing respect for the dead by avoiding displays of gaiety. But it is also likely that the custom is related to the primitive belief in disguising oneself after a death, to keep ghosts from recognizing and haunting one. Women's veils, in full mourning, seem most explicitly related to this ancient custom. It should be noted that people in other parts of the world prefer, or once preferred, brightness in mourning: the Burmese wear yellow, in parts of China white is worn, and in Persia traditional mourners wear sky-blue, to symbolize the spiritual realm to which the dead have departed.

Often it is considered lucky to give away your coloured clothing when assuming mourning; and of course in some European countries a widow may dress in the unrelieved black of mourning for the rest of her life. In the USA, though, it has been thought inadvisable to wear mourning for more than two years—or another family death would occur. Nor should black-edged paper be kept in the house after the period of mourning has elapsed. Gold ornaments should not be worn with mourning; mourning gloves must be cotton, or more deaths will follow, as they will if one puts on red clothing when coming out of mourning. And never kiss a friend through a mourning veil, or you will soon see him or her in mourning.

In preparing the corpse for burial, it was an ill omen if its eyes were found open: it was said to be looking for someone to join it in the grave. So in many places the eyes were held shut magically, as well as practically, by means of coins placed on them, which clearly descends from primitive customs of burying various goods (food, weapons, money) with the dead to assist them in the nether world. If a corpse is to be buried in a shroud, it

Dolmens like these in Ireland were built to keep the corpse from rising and to house its spirit. This was especially so in Teutonic cultures.

should be made of linen—for luck—and should have no knots or pins that might magically hamper the dead person in his progress towards immortality. A corpse should be laid in the coffin with its feet towards the east (symbolizing its eventual resurrection, like that of the rising sun). And the coffin must be carried through the *front* door of the house—an important point in country communities where that door was used only on ceremonial occasions. Also, the door must remain wide open until the mourners return.

Magical elements surrounding funeral processions have in some cases come to be accepted traditions for modern funerals, usually explained in terms of respect for the dead. Most of us know the unwritten rule against breaking into or otherwise interrupting a procession: in most cities, the cars in a procession are given the right-of-way, and will even go through red lights to keep up with the hearse. The tradition stems from the ancient belief that if the progress of the deceased to the grave is interrupted, the interruptor might attract the wrath of the ghost— or the ghost might be led to stay among the living, and haunt them.

It is widely considered unlucky to meet a funeral procession (especially for brides), or point at one, or allow a cat to cross the path of one. In parts of Britain, rainfall on the day of the funeral has been thought a good omen. It is bad luck to count the carriages or cars in a procession. Funerals must not be postponed, and a corpse must never be kept in the house over Sunday. It is believed best if the burial is held in the forenoon. A pregnant woman must not attend a funeral, nor should a mother carry an infant less than twelve months old in a procession: in each case the baby will die.

A common belief in Britain and Ireland states that the most recently buried corpse in a cemetery must act as the 'graveyard watcher'—guarding the cemetery, and summoning those of the locality who are to die. The watcher would be relieved of his duties when another burial occurred. This belief created problems when two funeral cortèges approached a cemetery at the same time. There would be a race, and often a pitched battle, to decide which corpse would avoid the onerous duty of watching. In some areas, varying the legend, the watcher

was thought to be the *first* person buried in a new cemetery; and often a sympathetic sexton would kill and bury a dog to provide the first corpse, for otherwise the first human corpse would have the job forever. Elsewhere it was said that the very *last* corpse buried, when the graveyard was full, would watch for all time; and then, too, the sexton might find some corner of an otherwise packed cemetery to inter an animal's corpse.

As for the grave itself, it should always be dug along an east-west line, and the body placed in it so that upon resurrection the dead could arise facing east—from which the Call will come. A grave must never be left open over Sunday. If the earth on a new grave sinks rapidly, another death will occur in the family. One must never step on the grave (a relic of the ancient fear of incurring the wrath of the dead): some American lore says that, if a grave is inadvertently stepped on, the offender must jump backwards over it to counteract the ill luck. Bad luck will follow if the grave is not ready when the procession arrives, for the same reason as the taboo against interrupting a procession. It is unwise to

These sixteenth-century tombs in Painswick, Gloucester, are Christian adaptations of earlier grave-markers.

In many cultures gifts were given to the dead to help them in after life. In this rationalistic age a wreath is the only survival of this custom, and is thought to 'bind' the dead spirit and prevent it from returning.

These are two woodcuts showing apparitions: the one nearest was seen in 1704, and foretold the result of the War of Spanish Succession. The other was seen in London in 1710.

remove anything, a flower, say, from a cemetery. And it is mortally dangerous to disturb a grave by disinterment or robbery, again because the ghost will exact revenge.

Some of the paraphernalia of burial deserve mention. The laying of wreaths descends directly from the primitive custom of giving gifts (usually of food) to the dead, and placing them on the grave, to appease and placate the ghosts. Some authorities suggest also that the wreath forms a 'magic circle' which binds the ghost and prevents it from returning.

The traditional hearse evolved out of a farmers' harrow—in fact, the word 'hearse' comes from an Old French word meaning 'harrow'. In medieval France the rake or harrow was suspended over the coffin as a makeshift chandelier, with the ceremonial candles impaled on the spikes. Soon, special constructions were being made, resembling harrows less and less, which were erected in churches to light and adorn funeral services. In a short while the harrow had become a platform on which the coffin rested; and then it was natural to begin using it to bear

The picture on the right shows the special rituals governing the burial of vampires. A stake was driven through the heart to pin them to the earth and they were buried at a crossroads to ensure that, should they return, the spirits would not know which road to follow to their old homes.

This old etching of the funeral of Queen Mary in 1695 shows bier-trappings very similar to the harrow which used to be suspended over coffins.

In some African funerals a mourner is hired to drive away evil spirits. They often wear masks to avoid being recognized by the spirits as does the one on the left.

the coffin to the grave. As wagons and carriages, and today motor cars, came to be adapted to functioning as hearses, most of the features of the original harrow have been lost entirely.

Tombstones, according to some folklorists, grew out of the primitive fear of the dead: the grave was weighted down with stones to keep the corpse from rising. But much more likely is the idea that such stones come from the ancient worship of stones, common in northern Europe millennia ago, and also found in other primitive cultures. Stones were believed to be the dwelling places of certain spirits; thus stones came to be used not only as markers for graves but as symbolic homes for the spirits of the dead.

Unnatural death—accidental or violent—creates an aura of superstitious fear in the living, for ghosts in this case are exceedingly likely to return for vengeance. For this reason executed felons were often buried at crossroads, partly because of the magical power of the cross in any form, partly because of the belief that the ghost would not be able to find the right road to its enemies. (Witches and vampires were similar-

This fourteenth-century woodcut shows a witch using hazel to cast a spell on a peasant. Hazel is perhaps the most closely associated with witchcraft of all magical trees.

This shows witches departing for a Sabbath, together with objects popularly associated with witchcraft.

ly interred, usually with a stake of some magical wood, or of iron, driven through their hearts to keep them in their graves.) In many parts of Britain, when a person died accidentally, or was killed outdoors and away from home, it was the custom to scratch a cross on the ground or on a nearby stone at the fatal spot—again in an attempt to 'lay' the ghost.

Suicides were also thought to be likely to return and haunt, and many of them were buried at crossroads as well. Or perhaps a suicide might be the one chosen to play the permanent part of 'graveyard watcher', as described above, since a suicide in the past seldom warranted a proper Christian burial.

Death by drowning has attracted much superstitious belief, presumably because of the old belief that such fatalities were caused by evil spirits of the water taking their victims. For this reason many superstitious people will do nothing to help a drowning person—though giving such help may be perfectly easy—for they believe that if the water is denied one victim

It always seems that women remember that taboo against opening an umbrella in the house!

Tam O'Shanter was pursued by one of the witches in her 'cutty sark'. She almost caught him, but running water is death to witchcraft and spells, and as Tam crossed the bridge she had to be satisfied with his horse's tail!

it will seek another. An allied belief states that if you rescue a drowning man he will be your lifelong *enemy*. When a drowned body is washed ashore, it must be buried within the tidemarks, for it has become the sea's 'own', and cannot be removed from its influence. To recover corpses of the drowned, searchers should place a lighted candle on a board and float it in a likely area. It will become fixed and motionless above the place where the corpse lies. A loaf of bread containing mercury will act in the same way. Some traditions say that a drowned person will rise to the surface in nine, or seven, days. And most agree that a drowned man floats on his face, a drowned woman on her back.

Understandably, death by drowning plays a prominent part in the superstitious beliefs of seamen. But then, as the next chapter shows, professional people in a great many walks of life are obsessed with their own forms of morbid fears, along with their own special versions of the magical ways to avert or overcome such terrors.

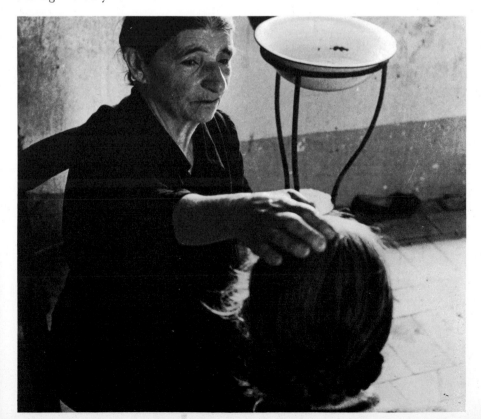

Raffaella Sinnopoli, one of the best-known witches in Southern Italy, can cure headaches, which she claims are caused by misfortune.

SUPERSTITION AT WORK

Leonard Bernstein always wears the same pair of cufflinks when conducting – presumably for luck. They were a gift from his mentor Serge Koussivitsky.

This wooden model from Papua (above) is thought to ensure good garden crops.

This Shinto shrine is travelling by ship round a bay in Japan, to appease the sea-gods and thus ensure good catches for the local fishermen.

names in many spells or incantations. The 'magic in a name' belief plays a part in the ritual of naming or 'christ-ening' a ship, which goes back to ancient times when the gods of the sea had to be propitiated before a new ship could be placed on the water. The traditional breaking of a bottle of champagne on the ship's bow descends from the old ritual libations to the gods—usually wine or oil, as with the ancient Greeks, but sometimes blood from a human sacrifice. And indeed, before champagne became popular in modern christening ceremonies, blood-red wine was commonly used.

Once at sea, sailors remained on the alert for any of a large list of omens, mostly bad. They feared a new moon on a Saturday, and a full moon on a Sunday. An albatross flying round the ship at sea presages bad weather or other perils ahead, though in some traditions it is a good omen. In either case it is fatal to kill an albatross (from which belief the poet Coleridge developed his *Ancient Mariner*), or to kill gulls, stormy petrels, and similar birds that follow ships to sea. It was felt that such birds were the spirits of drowned sailors, and should not be

harmed. Other birds, plovers, or cur-lews, or any sea-birds that emit a plain-tive whistling note, are called the 'Seven Whistlers', and their presence near a ship is an omen of disaster. Sharks persistently trailing a ship fore-shadow a death on board (the sharks, with foreknowledge, are supposed to be waiting for the body to be consigned to the depths). Rats, as everyone knows, are believed to leave a ship that is destined to sink, even when it still appears safe, or sometimes even before it sails. It is desperately unlucky if the ship's colours are torn, if anyone snee-zes on the port side, or if a mop and bucket are lost.

Probably the worst omen of all con-cerns one or another of the legendary 'phantom ships' that lurk on the high seas, of which the *Flying Dutchman* and the French ship *La Belle Rosalie* are perhaps the most famous. Such a ship will appear, in dangerous situations such as a storm or fog, at the moment when sailors must abandon all hope.

Taboos, as well as omens, crowd round sailors at sea. Priests and women are both considered unlucky aboard ship. Black objects are to be avoided when possible; pins and umbrellas are

unlucky. Among animals, hares, pigs, dogs and horses are unlucky, and so are cats on American ships. In connection with the dislike of carrying animals, Christina Hole tells the story of a ship that sailed in 1959 from the Antarctic to Norway, carrying a live albatross *en route* to a zoo in Germany. Shortly after sailing the bird died; and the ship then ran into storms, engine trouble and a host of other misfortunes, until the crew went on strike, unwilling to continue the voyage. In the end the ship staggered into Liverpool, its engines unable to complete the voyage—and the captain blamed it all on the albatross.

Also in 1959, after the *Queen Elizabeth* had met a series of delays, accidents and storms on a particular crossing, the crew decided that a pet budgerigar was the source of the ill luck, and refused to make the return trip with the bird aboard.

Worst of all company on board ship is a corpse. This is why a person who dies at sea is so often buried at sea. If a corpse must be carried, it must be placed so that it lies 'athwart', never parallel to the line joining bow and stern; and it must leave the ship at

These are two rainmakers in Aboriginal belief – Wuluwait and Bunbulama. This painting, made in ground-rock colours on wood, comes from Yirrkala, Northern Australia, and is used in rainmaking ceremonies.

96

In Northern Australia these elaborately-carved and painted totems seen on the right guard a man's grave, to appease the spirits attendant on his death and to form a dwelling-place for them, as well as to indicate the sacred spot to the rest of the tribe.

Below: H. R. H. Princess Alexandra launches the liner *Oriana* with the traditional bottle of champagne to 'placate the gods'.

the port before any living person.

Many sailors will not speak certain words while at sea, using circumlocutions when necessary. Taboo words include animals' names—hares and pigs, again, predominate here—and also the words 'drowning' (which would tempt fate), 'minister' or 'priest', 'church' or 'chapel', 'knife', 'salt', and for some inexplicable reason (in English tradition) 'eggs'.

Sailors still avoid cutting their finger-nails or hair during a calm at sea, for fear of raising a gale. To play cards at sea is unlucky: even if the crew dares to break this taboo, the 'devil's picture-books' will be thrown overboard (as they were by Columbus) at the

first sign of a storm. Salt must never be thrown overboard. Nothing should be lent from one ship to another, but if a loan is unavoidable, the article should be slightly damaged, rendered imperfect, to take off the curse. And a theft from a ship brings bad luck to the ship, unless the goods are recovered. A landsman should not point at a ship (pointing is associated with the evil eye). A sailor must never hand the ship's flag to another through the rungs of a ladder. He must never wear the clothing of a shipmate who has died at sea. He must never do any sewing or mending during a storm at sea—or he will prolong it, by 'sewing it on'. (So he should sew in fine weather.)

Above all, it is totally forbidden, even today, to whistle on board ship. Whistling, by sympathetic magic ('like causes like'), can raise a wind and may produce a gale. Whistling is also associated in folklore with summoning spirits. This is indicated by M. R. James's famous ghost story, firmly based on folk belief, entitled *Oh Whistle and I'll Come To You, My Lad*. But it is permissible, when a sailing ship is becalmed, to whistle very softly in order to produce a favourable wind.

Also useful in cases of becalming is the trick of speaking to the wind in coaxing terms. Or sailors can scratch the mast with their finger-nails, or burn an old broom, or throw overboard a broom without a handle. Children on board are lucky–and the British find luck in black cats. Sailors often wore plain gold earrings as amulets against drowning, and cauls (membranes that cover some babies' heads at birth) are effective for the same purpose. Horseshoes nailed to the mast prevented shipwreck in the days of sail, as did an old coin (preferably silver) under the mast. Naval salutes are usually in odd numbers, for luck. And many ships, especially American, have luck-bringing mascots on board.

The figureheads on old sailing vessels (probably derived from the ancient practice of dedicating ships to goddesses, for which reason, also, ships are called 'she') were believed to be in a way the repository of the ship's spirit. Without them, the legend runs, a ship cannot sink. Christina Hole describes an incident in 1928, when a film company hired an old schooner,

Greek pankratiasts, or wrestlers, of 400 BC,
(below) usually poured libations of wine and
oil to the gods before a bout (top).

At first the sailors feed the albatross; but
then the Ancient Mariner kills the bird and
decay and misfortune haunt the ship, according to the age-old superstition. These
etchings (bottom) by Gustave Doré, illustrate
Coleridge's poem.

The Flying Dutchman, a well-known omen
of disaster, appears to survivors of a wreck.

Sailors often blame bad luck on a particular
object or person, and are quick to remove
both. Jonah was the first person on record
to be so treated (below), when his ship ran
into a storm: we still talk of people round
whom bad luck centres as being 'Jonahs'.

without its figurehead, intending to
sink it for a scene in a film. Explosives
were set within the ship three times,
but it would not go down. Finally an
old sailor reminded the film–makers
of the superstition. The figurehead was
found and replaced, a fourth explo-
sion engineered, and the schooner sank
immediately.

Fishermen hold many of the superstitions of sailors, but add a few special-
ities of their own. (Here we are dealing with the crews of fishing vessels
that put to sea. The sporting fishermen, or anglers, will be considered later.) A fisherman will not set out to
sea if, on the way to his ship, he meets
a clergyman or a nun, or any drowned
animal. Scots fishermen expect ill luck
if they meet a barefoot woman with
flat feet; Cornish fishermen are wary
of meeting any woman; French fishermen fear only nuns and spinsters.
Throughout Europe fishermen dislike
being spoken to—even wished good
luck—on their way to the boats. British fishermen will not take a dog on
board, nor mention its name, nor that
of a rat. In some parts of Britain the
skippers of fishing vessels put an unac-
customed strain on the men by forbid-
ding all profanity on board ship.

The seaboots of a fisherman, when
carried by another, must always be
tucked under the arm, never carried on
the shoulder. A boat must never be
pulled from the water stern-first. It is
unlucky to repair and re-use a vessel
that has been wrecked and washed up,
and it is unlucky to break up an old
boat when it is no longer seaworthy.
It is unlucky, in some parts of Britain,
to burn fish bones, and to count the
catch (which will mean that no more
will be caught that day).

British fishermen consider it lucky
to find a bumble-bee on board; many

The Indonesian rice-dolly (left) shows how widespread the doll-traditions is. Below is a straw goat, or yule *Bocca*, from Sweden, symbolizing some of the old gods associated with winter rites. Here again, Christianity may have imposed this form on the devil in order to discredit the old gods.

European fishermen thrust knives into the masts for luck; it is good luck to carry salt in the pocket, and sometimes to salt the nets before they go into the water. An old British tradition says fishermen should beat their wives, for luck, before sailing. The inedible fish called 'fiddle-fish' in Britain bring good luck when caught, and usually they are towed behind the vessel until they fall to pieces—a belief that was reported still extant in 1949. Also, if the first fish caught at the start of the season is female, the fishing will be very good that year.

Fish themselves, in legend, are supposed to be both wise and prophetic. It is believed that they will desert a stretch of coastline where a murder or suicide has occurred. In Normandy, it used to be said that the fish left the coast when Napoleon fell (or, in another version, when the French monarchy fell). Fish are thought to bite well three days before a storm, but never on the day before a change in the weather. Large fish at the water's surface herald a storm, as do porpoises swimming rapidly southwards, or whales jumping.

Such beliefs concerning the weather, as has been seen, dominate sea-going superstitions. And many of them are well known on land. Most people share the belief, perhaps not wholly illogical, that seabirds flying inland provide a storm warning. And everyone must know the old jingle:

Red sky at night, sailors' delight.
Red sky in morning, sailors take
    warning.

Often shepherds or farmers, rather than sailors, are the subject of those lines, and sometimes it is a rainbow, not a red sky, that forms the omen. Naturally farmers and country people generally are as concerned with the weather as sailors, or perhaps more so today, when sailors need no longer worry about wind direction. It is, of course, impossible to do more than skim the surface of the immense subject of weather lore. But a few beliefs can be noted, as a representative sample.

Country people's weather lore depends a great deal on the actions of animals. In Britain rain is predicted by a cuckoo's persistent call; jackdaws fluttering round buildings; cattle lying on low ground; crickets chirping more loudly than usual; a rooster crowing

These cave paintings probably show that sympathetic magic was practised by the people who made them: the cavedwellers threw spears at the images to ensure that their spears would strike the actual animals. Even today some people think they can gain power over something by drawing it.

Sailors maintain that it is bad luck to move a beached wreck or a body: they both belong below the water line, once the sea has claimed them (bottom).

Sailors say that porpoises seen swimming southwards herald a storm.

Bottom left: early in the New Year, English farmers still bless the plough to ensure good crops. This is a remnant of more extensive pagan rituals – as is the Beating of the Bounds, another old rite now joyfully celebrated by the church at the beginning of May.

The familiar scarecrow may be another descendant of effigies of fertility deities connected with spring rituals.

from a gate; a cat sneezing; sheep bleating restlessly. In America, bad weather is foretold by the cawing of crows; fish biting eagerly in a stream; moles casting up more hills than usual; horses clustering in the corner of a field; bees staying in the hives; frogs croaking and donkeys braying excessively; swallows flying low, pigeons circling over water, and turkeys taking dust-baths.

Rain can be produced, either inadvertently or purposefully, by actions which include stepping on a black beetle, or a spider, or an ant; by cutting fern, or heather in parts of Brit-

ain; by sprinkling water on stones; by throwing flour into a spring (a ritual common in parts of France) and stirring it with a hazel stick. Fine weather can also be summoned, mostly by various incantations that rather resemble the familiar children's chant of, 'Rain, rain, go away: come again another day'.

To predict fine weather, look for bats coming out early in the evening, or livestock grazing peacefully; dandelions blowing out in the early morning; cobwebs on the grass in the morning; ants clearing their nests and pil-

ing up dirt; wild geese flying out to sea. Good summers can be foretold by rooks nesting high in trees, butterflies appearing in early spring, or (in Britain) oak trees coming into leaf before ash trees.

A hard winter is in the offing if nature seems to be preparing for it—by putting an extra thick skin on onions, or sending wild geese south in August; similar omens include extra down at the base of the feathers of domestic geese; thicker husks on corn; oysters bedding deep; squirrels storing an excessive amount of food.

This model of a dugong, or sea-cow, (right) is used in the Indian Ocean and surrounding areas to increase a fisherman's success. It is filled with a magic mixture of plants and dugong grease: after the original maker dies his leg-bones are attached to the charm to add to its efficacy.

The Congolese rainmaker below uses time-honoured charms and rituals to influence the weather.

As for the coming of spring, most countries have some sort of traditional omen centring on 2 February. On that day the hedgehog or badger (or, in North America, the animal called groundhog, or woodchuck) is supposed to come out of hibernation and look around. If he sees his shadow (i.e. if the sun is shining), he retires into his burrow, and winter will last for six more weeks. If no shadow is visible, spring is imminent.

A poor harvest is indicated by a full moon at Christmas, or rain on St Paul's Day (25 January). Other poor harvest omens include the evening star riding low in summer; a rake found lying with its teeth upwards; finding a ladybird (ladybug in North America) with seven spots or more on its back. A good harvest is foretold by a cuckoo calling from the south, in spring, or by an ear of corn with seven or fourteen rows. Sun on apple trees on Christmas morning presages a good crop the next year. And it is widely believed that 'a cold wet May means a barn full of hay' the following autumn.

Good harvests can be magically brought about by burning blackthorn and scattering the ashes over the first sowing of spring; or by having the local church bells rung at the time of reaping. The latter probably figures in the traditional harvest festivals that still continue in many parts of Britain and Europe, where the country folk gather to have fun but also to make a little ceremonial magic, ensuring the future fertility of their fields. British 'corn dollies'—vaguely mother-goddess images made from intricately woven grain stalks—still appear in these rituals, along with images of roosters similarly made. These figures represent the spirits of the harvest, the 'corn spirits', who are placated and coaxed to

The Valentine on the right, by Kate Greenaway, shows Cupid performing his customary function. Below, lucky horseshoes and nuggets attempt to persuade the visiting gambler in Las Vegas that luck is on his side.

Corn dollies now seem to be decorations: but they are probably descended from figures which featured in early harvest rituals as effigies of fertility gods. Several examples are seen in the two pictures on the right.

'Topping out' is still performed by the firm of Sir Robert McAlpine & Sons Ltd. Here the traditional everygreen bough is being nailed in place before toasts are drunk by contractors and clients. House-building rituals are recorded in many lands: this one is specifically North European (far right).

ensure good crops the following year.

Farmers know a host of superstitions in matters other than weather and harvesting. Some primitive magic to protect the fields can still be found: British farmers may erect little crosses of birch and rowan twigs; herdsmen prefer carrying sticks of ash wood, which keeps evil away from the cattle (and supposedly cannot injure the animals however hard they are struck). The familiar scarecrow, that straw-filled image of a man supported on a cross of wood, is just as much an offshoot of protective magic as it is a means of frightening birds away.

Upon seeing a hay wagon, country folk still make a wish—and some count thirteen first, one of the few *positive* occurrences of this number in folk belief. Hay stolen on Christmas Eve and fed to cattle will make them thrive. If fruit trees shed their leaves before autumn, the omen is bad, sometimes heralding an outbreak of cattle disease. Corn planted in the dark of the moon will have large ears low on the stalk. American farmers say one should never finish cutting corn before sunset; and one should hang a corn stalk over a mirror for good luck.

A number of beliefs featuring roosters has appeared in previous sections (in marriage divination, death omens, weather omens, etc.). Sometimes a rooster crowing on the doorstep (or entering the house) indicates a visitor coming. White roosters are invariably lucky, while black ones are associated with dark magic and evil. Some American farmers prefer to set eggs under hens on Sunday night, for successful hatching. They also believe that if thirteen eggs are set, twelve will be pullets and one a rooster.

Eggs are natural symbols of rebirth, which is why they form a part of our rather pagan Easter festivities. It is unlucky to take eggs out of the house, or sell them, after sunset—and unlucky to dream of them. Small eggs without yolks are bad luck; so is the sight of many broken eggs, or one soft-shelled egg. Eggs carried over running water will not hatch. The last egg laid by an ageing hen, or any egg laid on Good Friday, will make a useful charm to protect the henhouse.

Cattle have been sacred beasts in many countries other than India, as western folklore reflects. To make an offer for a cow that is not up for sale

On the eleventh day after Christmas apple trees were wassailed, and then fired on with blank charges. This odd custom was said to result in a good crop the following year.

Zsa Zsa Gabor always wears a valueless child's ring, a present from her grandmother, probably as a lucky charm. Sometimes objects or substances are lucky in themselves; or it may be that they have alway been associated with good luck by the owner.

is unlucky, and may bring about the cow's death. One must never strike a cow with the hand (which is sullying it with profane flesh). It is a good omen if cattle lie down on Christmas Day—and in parts of Europe it is still thought that cattle kneel at midnight on Christmas Eve, honouring the memory of the Bethlehem stable. Lanterns must never be placed on tables inside barns, or cows will lose their calves. It is ill luck for twin calves to be born. To touch a calf on the back will cause it to fall ill; to step over one, while it is lying on the ground, will kill it.

Farm animals must never be gelded under a waning moon; nor should pigs be slaughtered then (the meat will shrink when cooked), nor lamb's tails docked. The first lamb in spring provides a good omen if it looks at you, and also if it is black. More than one black lamb in a flock is unlucky. To meet a flock of sheep is a good omen, but one must never pass through it. Shearing sheep when the moon is waxing produces better wool. Dreaming of sheep foreshadows great pain.

Miners have many superstitions in common with seamen, as if venturing into the bowels of the earth demanded the same magic as venturing onto the bosom of the sea. So miners dislike meeting a cross-eyed person, or a rabbit, on the way to work; they too fear the birds called the Seven Whistlers. Miners will not say the word 'cat' within the mine—and any cat found there must immediately be killed. Like sailors, miners will touch iron to avert ill omens, but for them, understandably, coal has none of the power that it has for seamen and fishermen. As on board ship, whistling is absolutely taboo in a mine.

Miners, especially in Britain, know many omens of disaster. More accidents are said to occur when the bean plants are in blossom. A dove or robin flying round the pithead foretells disaster; miners still often refuse to work when such a bird has been seen. To dream of broken shoes indicates an imminent disaster. And many old miners still believe that washing the back (coal dust or no) will weaken it, and will probably also cause a collapse of the mine ceiling.

The profession of acting, and show business generally, may not seem particularly hazardous when compared to shipping or mining. But the success of

The patron Saint of vignerons, St Vincent, is carried through a town in the Burgundy region by the Chevaliers du Tastevin, to ensure a good vintage: this usually takes place at the end of January.

This is the figurehead of the *Joseph Conrad*, named after the famous writer of sea-stories. Figureheads were thought to embody the ship's spirit.

Blue and yellow predominate at this Chinese funeral in Singapore. Notice that faces are covered to prevent mourners being recognised by spirits, and also in token of grief.

Paul Anka (far right) is always careful not to go onstage until the first four bars of the introduction have been played.

This shrine of paper will be burnt to scare spirits away from the funeral and mourners (Singapore),

stage shows often seems to be as ascribable to good luck as to good management, and so theatre people are notoriously superstitious. Naturally, their beliefs are fairly specialized. Actors believe that three candles on stage or in a dressing room are unlucky, as are real flowers on stage during a performance. Cats are considered lucky around a theatre, but it is unlucky if one runs across the stage during a show. Peacock feathers or any representation of a peacock are taboo on stage. So is opening an umbrella, or dropping a comb.

Many theatre people dislike the colour yellow, and it must never be used for stage curtains. In the USA, some actresses fear that wearing black on stage means they will shortly be truly in mourning. It is bad luck to look over someone's shoulder into a mirror, so that both are reflected. Knitting is forbidden on stage or in the wings, because the magic of knots can 'tie' the show up. A cross-eyed person backstage is unlucky. Actors dislike wearing new clothes for the first time on an opening night; some variety performers like to continue wearing the same costumes that they wore when

they first tasted success. Spilling a make-up box is an evil omen. A drop curtain that forms a loop is bad luck; so is the fate-tempting act of peering through a curtain to see how large the audience is.

Whistling is as taboo in a theatre as it is aboard a ship. If someone forgets himself and whistles, even in the dressing room, he is sent out of the room to turn around three times and then beg readmittance. A British newspaper in 1958 reported that the troupe of dancers called the Tiller girls believed in this taboo: if any one of them whistled in a dressing room, it meant that the darkest girl nearest the door would lose her job. It is unlucky to speak the last line of a play at a rehearsal; a flawless run-through at rehearsal (again tempting fate) is unlucky. If an actor's shoes squeak as he makes his first entrance during a show, the omen is good. So it is if, in the dressing room, he kicks off his shoes and they land flat on their soles. Placing shoes on a chair or a shelf is bad luck. It is an evil omen if someone stumbles, or catches his costume, upon a first entrance—but it is good luck to fall, accidentally, during a performance.

Theatre managers and their 'front of house' employees have their own beliefs. Many managers will not open a show on a Friday. It is an omen of disaster if a woman faints, or someone dies, in the audience. A long run is assured if the person who buys the first ticket to a show is elderly—a short run if he is young. Receipt of a torn banknote at the box office is unlucky, and may mean a change of job for one of the employees. An usher is lucky if he seats the first arrival, but unlucky if he takes someone to a seat numbered thirteen, or if he misses the first words of the play, or if a woman buying a programme tips him. A tip from a man is good luck; and the first tip of the season is usually kept, as a lucky piece to draw more tips.

Practically everywhere in the world, theatre people are terrified of the play *Macbeth*. It is absolutely taboo to mention its name, and more so to quote from it, anywhere in a theatre or within the hearing of actors. (Some actors believe this superstition so deeply that they will even go to the length of turning down an offer of a part in the play.) Theatre tradition is rife with tales of disasters associated with *Mac-*

beth. For instance, in 1964 the new Portuguese National Theatre in Lisbon, built at a cost of about £700,000, burned to the ground a few hours after a performance of the play. And in 1967 a series of delays and misfortunes dogged the cast that was rehearsing the play in London's Royal Shakespeare Theatre—misfortunes including a hold-up of many weeks while the director recovered from an attack of shingles.

Only rarely are other plays considered dangerous in themselves. Among the traditional 'pantomimes' that decorate the London Christmas season (farcical musical versions of fairy tales and the like), *Cinderella* is considered lucky but *Robin Hood* and *The Babes in the Wood* are not. Several songs are avoided by show business people—of which, predictably, the Witches' Song from *Macbeth* is the most taboo. This song is believed to be the reason for the taboo against the play; it is sometimes thought to be able to summon evil spirits, through its very authenticity. 'I Dreamt I Dwelt in Marble Halls' was once considered ill-omened, but that is probably not the only reason for its lack of popularity today.

Singers and musicians, especially those who perform in show business, have few special superstitions of their own. But it might be noted that to them crickets and other 'musical' insects are sometimes believed to be good luck. And many popular musicians have lucky tunes, which they take up as their theme songs and make sure to play or sing at every performance. Classical musicians and composers seem relatively free from superstition, though, in some cases, if a musician is interrupted in the performance of a piece, he will consider it unlucky to pick up where he left off, and will instead begin something new. It is also worth noting that the composer Gustav Mahler, in 1907, gave his ninth symphony a special title, *Das Lied von der Erde*, rather than calling it, in the usual way, Symphony No. 9. He had learned that he was suffering from a heart disease, and he knew that Beethoven, Dvorak, Schubert and Bruckner had all died after writing their Ninth Symphonies (although Bruckner wrote ten symphonies, he numbered one of them No. O). In 1909, though, Mahler had recovered confidence enough to entitle his next symphonic work the Ninth.

Gamblers, in whose lives luck plays a

The two 'little people' in this moralistic etching above by Millais seem to be rejoicing at the gambler's bad luck. Perhaps he neglected the many superstitions surrounding gambling.

This scene from *Macbeth* features three witches in a cavern. The play's evil reputation may derive from its subject-matter, dealing as it does with the effect of evil and the 'ministers of darkness' on the human character.

central and basic role, seem to rely a great deal on the more common forms of superstition—the usual lucky charms and amulets, luck-bringing articles of clothing or habitual patterns of action. But they have some specialized beliefs as well—including the very common notion of 'beginners' luck', which will cause expert professionals to bet along with a novice to profit by his lucky innocence. Borrowed money is also lucky, which is why most gamblers will not lend money to another player—for they would be lending their luck. In Monte Carlo, if a suicide occurred of an unlucky loser, gamblers once believed it a propitious time to play against the bank.

Meeting a woman on the way to gamble is often thought unlucky, as is being touched by someone while play-ing, or having a cross-eyed person in the game. A loss of temper while play-ing is unlucky, as is singing during a game (especially at cards). To spoil an opponent's luck, wait till he has placed a used match in the ashtray, and then place another across his, thus 'crossing out' his luck. For a similar reason one must never gamble with one's legs crossed. In the USA, the receipt of a $2 bill when gambling is very bad luck. Gamblers will tear a corner off such a bill, to counter the evil, or, if the bill's four corners are already torn, destroy it. (This idea is said to spring from a common slang term for the $2 bill— 'deuce'— which is also a euphemism for the devil.) To be struck by bird droppings, especially from a pigeon, is good luck—ever since the last century when a man at Monte Carlo won heavily after a pigeon had soiled his hat.

Gambling with dice, especially in the American game called 'craps', has spawned a few beliefs, such as the crap-shooter's magical gestures when throwing the dice, of which snapping the fingers is the most common. Many crap-players talk to the dice, with the familiar 'seven come eleven' and other coaxing calls, which are magical incan-tations to make the dice obey. Crap-shooters will blow on the dice for luck, or rub them on a red-haired person, or rub them on their own thighs in an almost sexual gesture (and women often rub the dice on their breasts). These rituals seek to infuse some sort of magical essence into the dice, by contact with sources of power.

Meeting a frog in the road on your

Judy Garland always includes her theme-song 'Over the Rainbow' in her performance, for luck (left).

Women are unlucky for gamblers, but Mar-lene Dietrich seems to be doing her best for Destry (Brian Donleavy) in *Destry Rides Again*.

Monique van Dooren always carries a lucky gold-and-black dress with her when doing a show, even though she never wears it.

Winston Churchill pats his first horse, Colonist II, for luck. Colonist responded by winning 13 races in all – surely an example of beginner's luck!

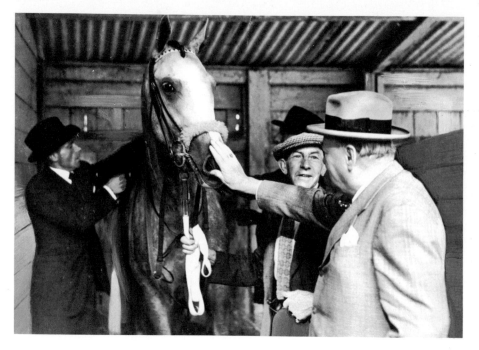

way to a dice game will bring you luck. Carrying dice means you will always have money. And finding a single die has definite omens: if it has one spot showing upwards, an important letter is coming. Two spots means a profitable trip; three spots, a pleasant surprise; four spots, bad luck; five, a change in domestic affairs and bad luck in love; six, excellent luck in all enterprises.

Card players (especially in poker) will not allow dogs at the table, nor will they play on a bare table, nor pick up cards with the left hand. Some will not touch their cards until the entire hand has been dealt; others insist on arranging their hands in special luck-bringing ways. As with dice, a loss of temper or singing are unlucky; so is dropping a card onto the floor. Someone looking over a player's shoulder or placing a foot on his chair brings him bad luck. Good luck is ensured if a friend inserts a pin in a player's lapel; or if the player (in poker) stacks his chips in a neat pile.

To overcome a streak of bad luck, poker players blow on the cards while shuffling, or get up and walk round their chair (or the table) three times in a sun-wise direction; or sit on a handkerchief; or turn the chair around and sit astride it; or bring out a new deck of cards. Some bridge players will stop the game if a black ace falls to the floor. Being dealt a long series of black cards is a death omen for you or a member of your family. Some North American poker players believe that cutting cards will cut off their

luck, or, as they put it, 'cut the cards and you cut your throat'. And, as everyone knows, to be lucky at cards is to be unlucky in love.

Of course individual cards serve as omens in the form of fortune telling called cartomancy, of which a small sampling might be given here. The ace and jack of spades are ill-omened cards, as are the jack and four of clubs and the deadly nine of diamonds. The ace of hearts is said to presage wealth; the two black jacks foreshadow poverty; the two red jacks indicate a hidden enemy. (But it should be remembered that these and other meanings ascribed to cards differ widely in various systems of fortune-telling.)

Betting on horses—the most popular form of gambling in the world—has evolved a host of obscure and often highly personal rituals, among betters, for picking winners. Many people jab a pin at random into the list of runners, trusting to the traditional virtue of the pin to guide them. Many choose their horses by the 'lucky' colours worn by the jockeys, or the lucky numbers that the horses carry. Others use complex systems of divination by numerology, astrology, dream interpretation and so on; still others search for good omens in horses' names. (And some spend immense time and effort studying form, learning all they can about breeding, trainers, jockeys, and race courses—yet seem to lose as often as the rest of us.)

Amulets are widely used among betters as well as among owners and jockeys. Several well-to-do British ladies

whose husbands had horses running in the 1967 Ascot admitted to buying entirely new ensembles to wear to the race, for luck, and some were in the colours of their jockeys. Some owners dislike being wished good luck before a race, and forbid anyone to whistle beforehand. Many owners (reportedly Bing Crosby among them) refuse to bet on their own horses. As for jockeys, it is bad luck for them to place their boots on the floor before a race. American jockeys will never touch brooms before racing. And, among amulets, it has recently been reported in Britain that a frog bone is still a favourite among jockeys and horsemen—as it has been since at least the Dark Ages.

Among players in sports other than the sport of kings, boxers and wrestlers are very given to the usual amulets and lucky charms. Georges Carpentier would never fight unless his manager was wearing a ragged old coat, which he had had for fifteen years. Bob Fitzsimmons kept a horseshoe nailed up in his training camp. Ezzard Charles once refused to enter the ring until someone had retrieved his 'lucky piece' —an old robe that his wife had thrown into the dustbin.

In golf, players also like to keep lucky bits of clothing, or old clubs. And many golfers will not clean the ball when a match is going well, nor will they approach the tee from the front.

Anglers have their good-luck charms as well, and in Sweden it has been noted that anglers believe no fish will be caught if a woman steps over the rod. Many fishermen will throw the

Bob Fitzsimmons, heavyweight champion 1897-1900, was one of a multitude of super-stitious sportsmen (left).

Ezzard Charles (below, right) lost this fight to Jersey Joe Walcott, in spite of the lucky robe he always wore at fights.

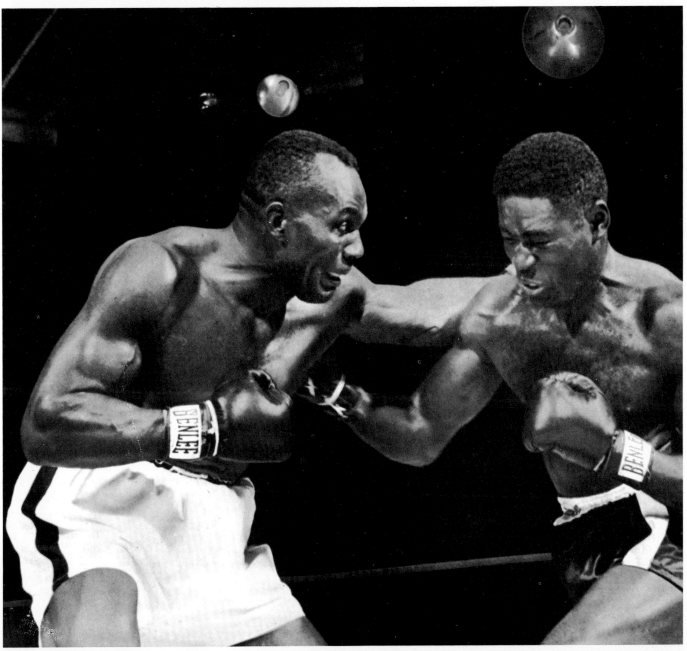

Puskas, Blackpools' mascot, did not manage to bring them luck when this picture was taken – despite his owner's fancy garb.

Below: Jackie Charlton is among those who always prefer to be last on the field.

first fish caught back into the water—to appease the water spirits? It is good luck to spit on the bait, and to put a lucky coin into the float. Never bait a hook with the left hand, or change rods while fishing, or tell anyone how many fish you have caught. Fishermen in a club in New Jersey, USA, always hang fish on a special tree before setting out—a magical ritual to ensure a good catch. And most fishermen agree that it is bad luck to sit on an upturned bucket. In Kent, in 1957, when some frogmen on salvage work ran into delay and trouble, local anglers ascribed their ill luck to the fact that one of them had used an overturned bucket for a seat.

In the sport of hunting, many participants say it is unlucky to turn back after having set out on a trip. It is bad luck to load your gun before reaching the hunting grounds, or to carry a gun on your left shoulder, or to place it on your shoulder indoors. It is good luck if your dog can be induced to fetch your game bag as you leave the house. A feather or a claw from your first bird makes a common amulet.

Team games breed their own special varieties of superstition among players, not only the usual amulets but also special rituals undergone during preparation for a game. In football (or soccer), so immensely popular in Europe, Britain and South America, preparation rituals among players have included a tendency to wear certain articles of clothing that had been worn when a winning streak began; a tendency to wait, before dressing for a game, until the bell summons the players onto the pitch; a tendency to put on the left sock, or boot, before the right, and so on. Many players, including Jackie Charlton of Leeds United, prefer to be the last player on the field—for luck. (This belief is said to have prevented Charlton from becoming the team captain: he would have had to *lead* the team out.)

And, of course, with football's focus on the feet, boots figure large in their rituals—as if they were trying to infuse a special magic into them before a game. For instance, in Britain, Nobby Stiles of Manchester United always leaves his laces undone until he is out on the field before a game. And Alan Gilzean soaks his boots in water before putting them on, perhaps thus achieving a tighter fit as well as good luck.

Gilzean, together with Robertson and Greaves, in action against Manchester United: his specially prepared boots seem to be standing him in good stead.

Nobby Stiles with his favourite suit, which he always wears when starting out for a game.

The Springboks brought over their own flag for the tour of Great Britain in 1951.

In Yokohama well-wishers pile flowers against a newly-opened store to bring it good luck. These undoubtedly are survivals of the sacrifices which would have been made in earlier times (far right).

Carlo Ubbiali of Italy retired safely after an extremely successful career in motor cycle racing. He is seen holding the sparking-plug he always carried with him for luck.

Far right: Hugo Koblet takes his wife for a ride on his birthday after the Six Day Cycle Race in Zurich, 1957. He would often tape a toy doll to his bike for luck.

The American national sport of baseball, with its vast following, has thrown up some special beliefs. The sight of a cross-eyed woman is unlucky; rubbing the head of a Negro bellboy in a hotel brings good luck, as does the sight of a truckload of empty barrels. (This last omen was born during the heyday of the old New York Giants: a series of victories was ascribed to the passing of such a truck, and so the manager had to pay a driver to bring a similar load daily past the ballpark, to keep his team's morale up.) A hat placed on a bed spells bad luck to a ballplayer, as does playing on Friday. Players will not use even a slightly damaged bat, nor will they lay bats crosswise. A dog on the field is a bad omen; a broken bat means bad luck for the batter, and spitting in the glove is a luck-bringing ritual.

Left-handed pitchers bring luck to a team, and it is widely believed among players and fans alike that a 'southpaw' is always eccentric. Above all, there is a universal belief that when a pitcher is well into a game and has not yet allowed any official hits, no one—neither players, nor the crowd, nor the people watching television at home—must mention aloud that a 'no-hitter' is being pitched. If someone does so, fate is tempted to thwart the achievement and the pitcher's luck will break. It is interesting that not even the opposing team—who should be anxious to break a no-hitter—will infringe this taboo.

This account of occupational superstitions can be concluded with some miscellaneous beliefs from various fields. For instance, in Britain butchers still often feel that women should not work in their shops, for a menstruating woman will taint the meat with her touch (an extremely primitive belief). Nurses in hospitals still refuse to allow red and white flowers together in a sick-room bouquet, for this combination is an ancient death omen. (An occurrence of this superstition was reported in a London hospital in 1965.) Also, if a nurse overturns a chair in a ward, she feels it means a new patient coming. Taxi-drivers feel lucky if their licence plate contains a seven, luckier if there are more than one seven, luckier still if the number contains a letter 'U', with its resemblance to a horseshoe.

Thieves say it is unlucky to steal from a church, and disastrous to steal the chalice of the Holy Communion.

Warren G. Harding (below).

Abraham Lincoln (below).

Franklin D. Roosevelt (top).

William McKinley (middle).

James A. Garfield (bottom).

John F. Kennedy.

They also will not steal playing cards, if they can avoid it. It is said that some burglars carry pieces of coal for luck; and in parts of Britain an old wives' tale states that carrying the dried heart of a toad keeps a burglar from being detected. The most familiar traditional way of avoiding detection involved the gruesome use of a corpse's severed hand—the 'Hand of Glory'. The thief must take the hand of a hanged felon, dry it until it hardens, then use it as a holder for a candle. Sometimes the candle must also be specially made, from ingredients that include a hanged man's fat. In a variant belief, the fingers of the hand itself were set alight. With the candle or hand aflame, no one in the house to be burgled could possibly awaken to catch the thief, as it were, red-handed.

Businessmen have a few beliefs of their own. If the first customer of the day (or the week, or the year) fails to make a purchase, it is a bad omen for business for the rest of the appointed time. In real estate, leases almost always run for an odd number of years, for luck; and of course 99-year

leases have the extra luck-bringing virtue of the magical number nine. Many businessmen dislike signing contracts, or beginning business trips, on the thirteenth of a month or on a Friday. Salesmen often keep articles of clothing—most usually ties—that they wore when they first became successful. Speculators who were born on 1 April (All Fools' Day) will be unlucky; those born on 29 February, in a leap year, will be lucky. It is good luck to begin a new business venture at the time of the new moon. And, in the USA, new businesses are often congratulated on their opening day by gifts of floral decorations in horseshoe shape.

Finally, a few beliefs centred around politicians. These gentlemen tend to rely more on public relations than magic of a more traditional kind, but some have been known believers in private omens and rituals. Perhaps the most superstitious politician of this century was the former Canadian prime minister, Mackenzie King. He not only dabbled in spiritualism, numerology, astrology and the rest; he had a host of small omens of his own invention,

such as the coming together of the hands of a clock, that lent added significance to important moments or decisions. Parnell, the great Irish patriot and statesman, apparently had a most unpatriotic belief in the ill luck associated with the colour green. He very nearly fainted at one public reception when some admiring ladies presented him with a green cap.

And there is a strongly-held belief concerning the American presidency. Ever since 1840 it has been said that presidents elected at twenty-year intervals, from that date, will die in office. Believers need simply point out that this has happened without fail since 1840. In that year William Henry Harrison was elected, and later died in office. So did Abraham Lincoln (elected in 1860), James A. Garfield (1880), William McKinley (1900), Warren G. Harding (1920), Franklin D. Roosevelt (1940), and John F. Kennedy (1960). Perhaps this string of facts does, after all, demand too much of our belief in 'mere' coincidence. Perhaps not. But it will worry many Americans during the election campaign of 1980.

Left: the figurehead of the *Spanish Lady*. Figureheads were thought to embody the 'spirit' of the ship, and were often female, although women on board ship have long been regarded as unlucky.

Below: sailors still refer to the bows of a boat as the 'eyes'. These originally represented the all-seeing eyes of the Egyptian god Horus, which would protect the boat. The idea has many parallels in Eastern myth.

During the last World War, many pilots decorated their planes with mascots to keep away gremlins and bad luck in general.

SUPERSTITION AND CATASTROPHE

If superstition and magic are bred as much, or more, out of fear as out of hope, then that breeding must be vastly magnified during times of great fear, especially of mass fear. Undoubtedly this is exactly what happens. A community is never so superstitious as in those times when calamity, either natural or man-made, threatens its existence. Even the most rational men, at such times, can feel the old atavistic terrors stirring, in the face of the inexplicable and the inevitable. The circumstances of disaster are beyond human control, in the ordinary way, and certainly beyond individual control. So the paraphernalia of magic (as well as of religion) are revived, or strengthened where no revival is necessary.

Superstition naturally offers some means of prophesying disaster. In areas that live with the constant possibility of flooding, a flood will be foreseen if two full moons occur in one month, or if the new moon appears 'on its back', that is, with the horns pointing upwards. This latter belief depends on the idea that the moon's crescent in this position is 'full of water', which will eventually spill over and inundate the land. Yet, to some people, the moon in this position signifies *dry* weather approaching, on the principle that the moon's curve catches the rain and keeps it off the land. Some areas of America, in a belief dating from pioneer days, believe that if you can hang a powder-horn on the moon's crescent, dry weather will follow; if you cannot, which means the crescent is upright, the land will be deluged by the water 'spilling out'.

Some Americans also see a flood warning if a cat lifts a paw above its ear three times in a row—or if a cat washes itself excessively, particularly its ears. In Illinois it is said that if a flock

W. Small's illustration to *The Star*, by H.
G. Wells, shows the awestruck fear still
produced by irregularities in the sun, moon
and stars.

Below: the holy rock, or K'aaba, at Mecca,
was thought to have fallen from heaven,
and thus to be of immense power.

These grief-stricken Peruvians believed that an evil spirit was swallowing their moon.

Meteors – or thunderbolts, as they were called – were always regarded as horrible potents. Here two men are seen digging one up in 1628. One has already fainted with fright!

of wild geese, flying west, does *not* veer north or south upon coming to a town, a great flood will occur within a few days.

Animals also provide omens of approaching famine. If crows, robins or rooks desert a favourite wood, *en masse*, the locality is facing a time of want. So it is if two crops of fruit have been taken from the trees in one year—or if the harvest in general has been exceptionally, perhaps unnaturally, rich. Here the principle is the temptation of fate: you may get bumper crops one year but you pay for them with short crops the next.

In those parts of the world where hurricanes are a constant danger, they are foretold by the appearance of a golden ring round the moon. (Long-fellow used this omen in his poem *The Wreck of the Hesperus*.) In tropical areas, a hurricane is foreshadowed by a small, fast-growing black cloud that is in violent motion. Now meteorologists might be able to find some logical connection between these signs and the great destructive winds. They would not, however, in the case of some ideas that are still current in the 'tornado belt' of the USA. There, for instance, it is said that if hogs gaze continually at the sky (when nothing is there to draw their attention) a tornado is coming—as it is if crows begin flying about erratically, in a kind of hysteria. In some midwestern areas, the very word 'tornado' (or 'cyclone') is taboo, in that the wind will be summoned when its name is spoken.

Rings around the moon, although due to special weather conditions, have always been feared as omens of bad luck – especially if they appear on the 13th day of the month, as this one did.

In 1877, Turks fired on an eclipse of the moon to frighten away the evil spirit responsible for it.

For those people who live in fear of the earth moving, the best known sign of an imminent earthquake is extreme restlessness on the part of domestic animals, especially cattle. Wild animals, too, are sometimes thought to foreshadow earthquakes by their actions. For that matter, there have been many people credited with a special extrasensory perception that allows them to foretell earthquakes. The ancient Greek hero Theseus claimed this power, due to his special relationship with Poseidon, who was god of the sea but also was called 'shaker of the earth', and who often appeared in the form of a bull (connecting with the cattle superstition mentioned above).

Earthquakes themselves, incidentally, figure in some interesting supersti-

tions. To dream of one, for instance, indicates that the dreamer should be cautious in his waking affairs. And an old British rhyme sets out some omens drawn from earthquakes' occurrence:

There are things
An earthquake brings:
At nine of the bell
They sickness foretell;
At five and seven they betoken rain;
At four the sky
Is cleared thereby;
At six and eight comes wind again.

Epidemic, plague and pestilence are foreshadowed, in British lore, by the unexpected blooming of violets in autumn, or by the sudden withering of bay trees. (The latter also presages the

death of kings.) In parts of the USA, the appearance, fortunately fairly rare, of a white comet indicates the coming of pestilence.

Of course, the great awe-inspiring cosmic fireworks—the shooting stars, meteorites, eclipses, comets and so on—would understandably spawn the deepest terror in primitive minds. Such phenomena happened infrequently, and so could never become familiar; and they occurred in the distant heavens, the realm of the gods. It was not difficult for men to assume that they were special visitations, special displays of the wrath and power of the gods, and that they foretold all sorts of mighty and far-reaching events, mostly catastrophic.

'Falling stars', those bits of space-

Wunder-Ey.

Welches den 12. Decembris dieses mit G.Ott zu Endlauffenden 1680. Heil-Jahrs zu Rom / von einer Henne mit grossen Geschrey ist geleget / und von hoher glaubwürdiger Hand solcher Gestalt in den Entwurff und Abriß gebracht worden.

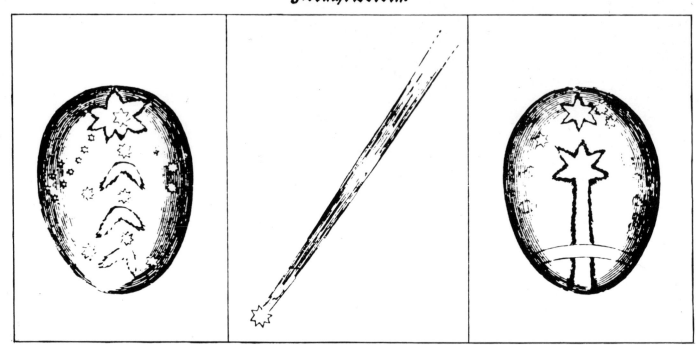

This German pamphlet of 1680 shows an egg with comet-like markings on it which gave rise to much speculation and alarm, especially when Halley's Comet appeared later that year.

travelling rubble that blaze up upon entering the earth's atmosphere, have long been associated with departing human souls, and so have been taken as death and general disaster omens. Meteorites, falling on the earth, have actually been worshipped in various parts of the world, including India, Japan, Siberia and pre-Columbian America. Several of the sacred statues of ancient Greece, including the Venus of Paphos on Cyprus, were carved from meteoritic rock. The holy black stone in the Islamic shrine called the Ka'aba, which all Moslems hold sacred, is said

to have been from a meteorite. And history tells us that in 1492 a meteorite fell in Alsace (then in German hands) and was taken by the Emperor Maximilian as a sign of his forthcoming victory in a war with France.

Eclipses of the moon or sun strike special terror in primitive minds, presumably because the watchers see them as an evil force devouring the heavenly bodies. Usually, in ancient history, eclipses signified the death of kings, and fortune tellers can cite many cases where the omen proved true. For example: in AD 59, after an eclipse

This is Halley's Comet, which, even in 1910, created much fear and rumour! In 1680, plagues, wars and general catastrophes were announced when it appeared.

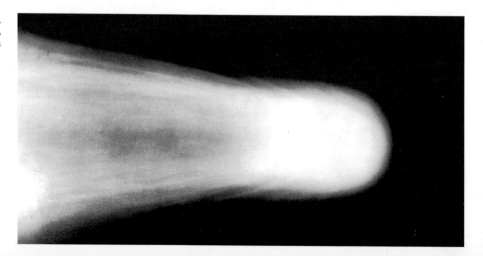

Magic is often a last resort in times of stress. In spite of strong commands to the contrary, Saul asked the Witch of Endor to help him before his last battle. At her bidding, the ghost of Samuel appeared and foretold his defeat at the hand of the Philistines.

Drake's Drum is said to sound when England is in danger, to summon his ghost. It was probably beaten in 1596 when he was buried at sea.

of the sun, Agrippina was murdered by Nero. In 1536 an eclipse was followed by the death of Queen Catherine of England. Other disasters have been superstitiously associated with preceding eclipses: a war in Persia in 463, the Black Death of 1348, fearful hurricanes in the West Indies in 1781, Napoleon III's war on Prussia in 1870, and, some mystics insist, the start of World War I.

In the eighteenth century the whole of London was thrown into turmoil by a prediction that issued from a prominent astronomer (and astrologer), William Whiston. He foretold that an approaching eclipse of the moon would be accompanied by the appearance of a comet which would herald the end of the world. His words were widely publicized, and caused a city-wide panic when the comet duly appeared near the appointed time. Thousands of Londoners fled from their homes; there were riots, stampedes and overall hysteria for many days.

Comets above all are fearful omens, largely because they appear even more infrequently than eclipses, and because to a superstitious mind they vaguely resemble a divine weapon—a spear or

arrow or similar missile. When a comet appeared over America in 1680, the fire-and-brimstone puritan preacher Increase Mather used it in a sermon: 'As for the sign in heaven now appearing, what calamities may be portended thereby...? In general we have cause to fear that sweeping judgments are thereby signified... I am persuaded, that the floods of great water are coming...'

A comet, to Mather, signified a terrible flood. Other people, at other times, foresaw equally dire calamities. A comet of 1066 was believed to be an omen of the Norman invasion of Britain. In 1214 another (or, indeed, perhaps the same) comet appeared, and on the day it disappeared Pope Urban IV died. In 1628 European star-gazers argued fiercely over exactly what was foretold by the comet then passing over them. Most plumped for general pestilence, and were partly justified in 1630 when plague decimated the city of Milan. In 1680 Europe was once more agog about a comet, the same one on which Mather preached, and much publicity was gained by a hen's egg laid that year with vaguely comet-like markings on it. In 1832 astrono-

mers started something of a grass-fire panic with an announcement that a comet would intersect the plane of the earth's orbit. It took some time to get it through to the hysterical people that the earth would not in fact be *at* that point in its path during the moment of intersection.

Nor has the irrational fear of comets died entirely—as many of us will be able to note in 1987, when Halley's comet once again visits us on its seventy-six-year cycle. A good deal of fear and superstition was generated on its last tour, mostly due to the still flourishing belief that comets presage war. And perhaps World War I followed soon enough to enhance those beliefs.

The beautiful appearance of the Aurora Borealis, or 'Northern Lights', has also been drafted into the employ of the superstitious, again as a widespread omen of war. Of course in northern climes such a belief has gained no foothold, for there the sight is too common, on a clear winter night. But further south, where the Aurora is rarely seen, the fear finds fertile ground. Nor has it lost popularity in recent times. In 1939, when Britain was hurtl-

This spread from 'Griff and the Gremlin', (right) a wartime publication, shows two of the faults blamed on this ubiquitous and evil little creature of RAF mythology.

These American airmen (centre) dangle their mascot beside the bomber named after it.

Louis de Wohl was employed by the British Government during the last war, to inform them what advice and information Hitler would be receiving from his astrologers. The Fuehrer relied heavily on astrological advice to determine the timing of vital enterprises.

Magnetic compasses provide
A home for Gremlins V inside
Their horrid habits lead to terrors
Like odd acceleration errors.

Der Hamburg, ringed by big balloons,
The Mark IV Gremlin flits and moans
Its eager horns hook in your fin
And 'mongst the cables drags you in.

14

15

ing downhill towards war, the Aurora was seen as far south as London. And in the USA, just before the Japanese attacked Pearl Harbour, magnificent displays were seen for three successive nights, as far south as Cleveland, Ohio.

But more commonplace occurrences —or at least those involving more commonplace things—can also serve as omens of war. Once again animals figure largely. Americans say that war is heralded by the appearance of a great number of locusts, with the curious markings on their wings vaguely resembling a W. (But some say the letter stands for 'want', or famine. And if a P can be seen in the markings, peace will come.) An over-large yield of lambs in the sheep flocks signifies war, as if nature were preparing for a period of hardship; and a great increase in the number of rats means the same. Again, when ants are plentiful and extremely active, war is foretold. Conversely, so it is when bees are strangely idle, or unsuccessful in their honey production. The appearance, in Britain, of an unusually large number of waxwings is a war omen. In Sweden the appearance of a hoopoe indicates war; elsewhere, the omen is clear if ravens are seen flying towards one another, or if eagles fly low over the valleys and plains.

War is heralded, too, when newly born male babies considerably outnumber females—and also when children begin to play soldiers in the street. A dream of blood foretells war. In celestial terms again, a red moon means war, as does the sight of a strange 'heart-shape' in the north-

The Romans used haruspication, or divination based on the position of a bull's entrails, to guide them in affairs of state.

This (centre) is an artist's impression of the (entirely fictional) angels which were said to have appeared in August 1914 to Allied Forces in Mons.

This young Ghanaian stabs himself to prove the power of the Ewe god of war (bottom).

western sky, with stars visible within it. Also, in parts of the USA, it is said that the disappearance of a particular group of seven stars (unspecified) signifies war. And, on a positive note, it can be added that the appearance of a complete rainbow at times of international crisis is an omen of peace.

The importance of war in superstition may be indicated by the existence of some very special, and unlikely, omens. For instance, several British bodies of water act strangely before a war. Assenden Spring, in Oxfordshire, notoriously irregular in its flow, runs full before a war; locals swear it did so in 1914 and again in 1939. A well called St Helen's, in Staffordshire, dries up before wars and other calamities. A dry pool in Devon is said to fill before a national catastrophe, and is said to have done so shortly before the death of King George VI in 1952.

The British also know of a marvellous drum, said to have belonged to Sir Francis Drake, which emits a long roll—by itself—to prophesy war, and is said to have done so in 1914. Apparently it also heralds victories, for Christina Hole notes the modern legend that the drum rolled in 1918 when the German fleet surrendered at Scapa Flow.

To match these, from American history comes a remarkable belief that, during the Civil War, stripes of red, white and blue manifested themselves in the night sky before major battles.

The awful trauma of war itself, as it sweeps a nation, produces an understandable mass urge for any or all forms of reassurance—and also prod-

A view of the aurora borealis, a phenomenon caused by the sun's emission of self-luminous particles. Violet, green, purple and rose are all colours commonly seen in this display. Also called the Northern Lights, it was thought to foreshadow evil and destruction.

Below we can see the comet which appeared before the Norman invasion of Britain, recorded on the Bayeux tapestry; Harold is clearly worried. Comets and unusual stars have always been of great significance: for instance, it has been calculated that a major conjunction of stars must have occurred at Christ's birth, giving the appearance of a new, enormous star.

William the Conqueror showed his face during the Battle of Hastings, to re-assure his followers that he was still alive, in spite of the fact that he had stumbled on landing, and was rumoured to be dead as a result of this bad omen.

These Simba rebels in the Congo queue patiently for a blessing from the witch doctor Mama Mary, before going into battle during the Congolese revolt, 1964.

uces a wide assortment of mass delusions, born of an anxious populace grasping at supernatural straws. Nothing else can explain the incredible boom in astrology and similar forms of pseudo-scientific prediction that accompanied the outbreak of World War II. It was a boom that sparked a demand in the British House of Commons for muzzling the astrologers, who were so frequently predicting a quick victory for the Allies that at least one MP feared for the country's war effort. There was no doubt—as mass opinion polls indicated—that millions of people had begun to take fortune-telling desperately seriously in the early 1940s.

More localized delusions have been fostered by the tensions of war, of which it is worth mentioning the widespread 'half-belief' (often rather more than half) among airmen, that faults and disasters in aircraft were caused by mischievous beings called 'gremlins'. These and allied creatures were merely the latest of a long line of 'Little People', prominent in European legend, who seem to devote themselves to making life miserable for humans. Pilots in the Allied forces had many magical means of circumventing the gremlins' activities: among them, a belief that an empty beer bottle proved irresistible to them—they crept inside and stayed out of mischief.

In certain coastal areas of Britain, during World War I, it was firmly believed that the ghosts of seamen killed in action were playing their part in the battle. The legend says that strange lights were flashed on the British coast, visible only to enemy ships, which lured those ships onto the rocks, rather in the way that criminal gangs a century or two earlier wrecked ships to loot them.

But, also from that war, perhaps the most famous mass delusion came from an unusual turnabout, the alteration of outright fiction into accepted fact. An English writer named Arthur Machen, then unknown but now (posthumously) revered as a master of fantasy fiction, wrote a short story in which the flagging spirits of British soldiers at Mons, in Belgium, were revived by the appearance of angelic warriors in

This Ching cat carved from teak is the emblem of the South Staffordshire Regiment. It was presented to the regiment in 1925, at Mandalay.

Winston Churchill breaks ranks aboard H.M.S. Prince of Wales, August 1941, to touch a black cat for luck.

Military standards, as well as these personal ones, are often hung in churches and cathedrals; they make an interesting blend of war and the supernatural.

the sky, urging them on into battle. It is a fairly common motif in folklore: that such divine aid was often forthcoming (to those on the right side) at moments of great need was accepted by many Christians in earlier centuries, among them St Thomas Aquinas. But the story set the country afire—and in the process its fictional nature was forgotten. People readily believed that the angels of Mons had been seen; soldiers and others immediately came forward claiming to have been eyewitnesses, and adding their own flourishes to Machen's original; earnest pamphlets were written analysing the meaning of the manifestation in terms of Britain's possible victory. (It should be added that Machen's role in the drama was promptly forgotten, and that he remained as unknown and unsuccessful as he had been before.)

In a wartime atmosphere of anxiety and delusion, the more familiar superstitions can gain extra footholds on the minds of the people at home. During World War II, soldiers' wives came to believe it was taboo (tempting fate) to refer in conversation to their husbands' leave. In munition factories, workers scrawled the names (or caricatures) of enemy leaders on bombs and shells. (Names have always figured in magical charms; so have images.) People with relatives in the forces went to great lengths to prevent the occurrence of the best-known death omens: for instance, by keeping dogs indoors at night so they could not howl near the house. Families set extra places, on special occasions, for husbands or sons fighting abroad. The authorities

Roman Legion and Cohort standards are examples of the standards round which troops were rallied during tense moments of battle. Also, as the identifying sign of one's cohort, they were felt to embody the group's spirit. It was a terrible dishonour to lose one in battle.

This handsome goat is now the mascot of the Welsh Regiment, and is one of the famous Cashmere goats established in Windsor Park, 1828. He is traditionally called 'Taffy'. Also seen here are the Goat Major, Commanding Officer, and escort of drummers.

warned people against talking in public about the whereabouts or doings of their loved ones in the forces, but superstitious people made such topics more or less taboo anyway, in fear of somehow jeopardizing the positions of the soldiers.

In Britain, the unlucky number thirteen had a brief moment of glory. Bus drivers on route number 13 in London maintained a non-stop service throughout the fearful blitz of 1940, and many felt that the number had kept them safe from bombs. Once the USA had entered the war, superstition there became so rife that the War Production Board grew worried. The Board declared superstition 'unpatriotic', and backed a campaign by match manufacturers to make it clear to the public that the refusal to light three cigarettes on one match was a waste of valuable paper, lumber and glue.

But of course in wartime the real hotbeds of superstition are the armed forces themselves. Men facing combat understandably collect just about every device they can think of that might confer some reassurance, and included among the devices are not only the accepted religions, but various kinds of philosophic fatalism. It was a common belief in World War II that you would not be killed in battle until your 'number' came up. This was predetermined, and so was not to be worried about. A similar insulation against anxiety came from the widespread notion that only *one* enemy bullet or shell had a soldier's 'name on it' (compare the ritual among munition workers, above); somehow this idea prevented soldiers

Another bomber mascot from World War II.

as did the sailors mentioned earlier. And of course the worst possible omen is the loss in battle of flags, banners, regimental colours, and the like. This superstition is related to the primitive belief in 'totem' magic: the totem, usually an animal or, of course, its image, was considered in a way to possess the spirit of the tribe. Harm done to it harmed the entire tribe. So the loss of the colours not only injured the regiment's honour, but struck magically at its unity and very existence.

Protective magic truly came into its own during World War II. A group of American social psychologists, in a detailed study of US servicemen, noted the most prominent magical practices: the usual amulets carried into battle, including the ubiquitous rabbit's foot, but also crosses and Bibles; various taboos, against three cigarettes on a match or against tempting fate by laying plans for peacetime; fixed patterns of action in pre-combat preparations; articles of clothing or equipment endowed with power by being associated with past escapes from danger.

A Dutch psychologist, J.A.M. Meerloo, wrote during the war: 'We all went into war with amulets and mascots, convinced that while we possessed them we could not be harmed. We also made use of magical formulae which took away fear.' He noted a formula, or incantation, which he himself used while a prisoner of war: he would repeat, over and over like a chant, 'It is philosophically absurd to end my life at this very moment'.

The novelist John Steinbeck, serving as a war correspondent, reported in the *New York Herald Tribune* some of the amulets he noted among the forces. A soldier might carry a smooth stone, an oddly shaped piece of metal, lucky coins, rings or other jewellery associated with people at home. Sometimes even photographs of wives or parents became magical, like the other objects, by being associated with lucky escapes from harm. One soldier carried a small wooden carving of a pig, which he spoke to—'Pig, this is not for us'—in moments of danger.

Folklore traditionally associates several objects with protecting soldiers in battle—lumps of coal, amethysts, even a preserved caul purchased from its owner (a process mentioned in Chapter Two). But most soldiers devised their own amulets, and found other ways to ensure their luck. In World War I,

from becoming panicky about *every* bullet.

Anxiety tended to be increased, however, by certain omens of disaster and defeat in battle. It spelled bad luck if a soldier stumbled as he went into battle. Airmen believed they would not return from a mission if they made their beds before leaving. (An unmade bed indicated that its owner would return to sleep there again. Similarly, it was lucky to shave before a mission: you would thereby get back for an evening's entertainment.) Many birds provide fearful omens: the ancient Romans feared, among other signs, the appearance of vultures over their legions when they were marching towards a battle. And in many parts of the world today birds of prey, especially hawks, seen flying to the left of an army indicate defeat. British soldiers once feared the whistling birds known as the 'Seven Whistlers' as much

In 1952 the British Government brought in witch doctors against the Mau Mau threat. They administered an oath on the 'Death Stone' which was powerful enough to cleanse those Kikuyu who had previously been forced to swear the Mau Mau oath in blood. Left, the witch doctor is thrusting symbolic arrows into the Death Stone. Above, at a later stage, a subject is individually cleansed from the evil associated with the oath.

Agnes Sampson and her witches' coven raising a storm against the King's Ships, 1591. This woodcut shows how strong was the belief in, and fear of, witches. The last legal hanging of a witch in England took place in 1722; but even after 1736, when the laws against them were repealed, there were many who advocated their death.

for instance, gunners on a particular battery found that unpleasant things happened whenever a novel by Rider Haggard was included in a box of books sent to them. So from then on they burned every book by that author that arrived.

Nor were superstitions found only among enlisted men. Officers and leaders succumbed as well. Hitler, of course, was notoriously given to such beliefs: he and some of his general staff paid close attention to astrological predictions during the war. And Hitler also had confidence in the luck-bringing power of the number seven. Sunday, the seventh day of the week, thus became an auspicious day in his eyes—and so his major attacks on Austria, Poland, the Netherlands, Yugoslavia and Greece, and Russia, were each launched on a Sunday.

In the Allied Forces, General Eisenhower himself was said to carry a particular gold coin as a lucky piece. And Lt.-Gen. George C. Kenney of the US Fifth Air Force carried a pair of dice, which had been acquired in Paris and blessed by a priest with the proviso that they should not be used for gambling. It was said that before a successful attack against the Japanese on Rabaul, in the Pacific, Kenney rolled the dice for an omen—and they came up lucky eleven.

Perhaps the clearest indication of the hold that magic had over the Services comes from the prevalence of mascots, living animals, owned by particular units. (Here, even more than in the case of the colours, the 'totem' connection is clear.) Of course at times the mascots also had duties to perform, if for instance they were dogs trained in

Another RAF mascot from World War II.

Three suns appeared on Charles II's birthday on 19 November 1648. Six weeks ater, on 30 January 1649, he was executed.

rescue work. But many mascots were merely pets—unusual ones, sometimes—and repositories of the group's luck. There are the goats belonging to the Royal Welch Fusiliers in Britain, and the wolfhounds of the Irish Guards. There were also the lion mascot of a Royal Canadian Air Force squadron, the donkey of the US Eighth Air Force, the rabbit of the HMCS *Haida* (in spite of the old sailors' taboo), the canary on a British troop ship, the goose of a Desert Air Force unit at Tobruk, and the Himalayan bear that belonged to another RAF squadron.

But many servicemen's mascots remain in that position during the unit's rôle in peacetime, when the men have no urgent need to ensure their protection from harm. So the 'totem' role of these creatures (as of the mascots of athletic teams) is underlined, because they are permanently a part of the units. It perhaps goes to show that, while superstition multiplies startlingly when people find themselves *in extremis*, it does not dwindle or wither away to a corresponding degree in more settled times.

And it might therefore be concluded that man is to a large extent a perennial pessimist, always believing that fate or bad luck or some evil spirit is waiting to crush him, always searching for more and more ways to stave off the moment of disaster.

Future folklorists will undoubtedly not lack for material, to form new collections of superstition. Their only problem may be to comprehend what new forms the ancient beliefs and rituals have taken as men adapted themselves to new environments.

ACKNOWLEDGMENTS

Aldus Books; H. R. Allen; Arts Council of Great Britain; Ashmolean Museum; Associated Press; Barnaby's Picture Library; Michael Busselle; Camera Press; M. Hassan & *The Observer*; J. Allan Cash; Central Press; Crown Copyright, Central Office of Information; Mary Evans Picture Library; Forget-me-not Cards Ltd; F.P.G.; Fox Photos; John R. Freeman; French Government Tourist Office; Philip Gendreau; Giraudon; Will Green; Hamlyn Archive; Michael Holford; Robert Indge; A. F. Kersting; Keystone Press Agency; Keystone View Co. of New York; Kobal Collection; L.E.A.; Peter Larsen; Maurice Lenssens; Frederic Lewis: Ed Carlin, Herbert, Thomas Muir; Harold M. Lambert; London & Manchester Assurance Co. Ltd; Sir Robert McAlpine & Sons Ltd; R.B. McLaughlin; Mansell Collection; Mount Wilson Observatory: Musée de l'Homme; Napper, Stinton & Woolley; National Gallery, London; National Museum of Finland; Photo Researchers: Bisserot, Jane Burton; Photo Researchers, New York: Van Bucher, Sid Latham, Joe Munroe; Pictorial Parade; Pictorial Press; Pilot Press; Axel Poignant; Paul Popper; Press Association; Publifoto, Milan; Radio Times Hulton Picture Library; Christopher Ridley; Royal Shakespeare Co.; Savoy Hotel; Bob Schalkwijk; Syndication International; The Times; Topix; U.S.A.F.; U.S.I.S.; Victoria & Albert Museum; Wartski; John Webb; Wellcome Historical Medical Museum: H. Meyerowitz.

INDEX